CONNAUGHT

TRAVEL GUIDE

MADEIRA

CHRISTOPHER AND MELANIE RICE

★★★ Highly recommended
★★ Recommended
★ See if you can

This edition is published by Connaught
an imprint of New Holland Publishers Ltd
First edition, published in MMIII
London • Cape Town • Sydney • Auckland
10 9 8 7 6 5 4 3 2 1

website: www.newhollandpublishers.com

Garfield House, 86 Edgware Road
London W2 2EA, United Kingdom

80 McKenzie Street
Cape Town 8001, South Africa

14 Aquatic Drive, Frenchs Forest,
NSW 2086, Australia

218 Lake Road, Northcote,
Auckland, New Zealand

ISBN 1 84517 014 8

Although every effort has been made to ensure that
this guide is up to date and current at time of going
to print, the Publisher accepts no responsibility or lia-
bility for any loss, injury or inconvenience incurred
by readers or travellers using this guide.

Keep us Current
Information in travel guides is apt to change, which
is why we regularly update our guides. We'd be
grateful to receive feedback if you've noted something we should include in our updates. If you have
new information, please share it with us by writing to
the Publishing Manager, Globetrotter, at the office
nearest to you (addresses on this page). The most sig-

nificant contribution to each new edition will receive
a free copy of the updated guide.

Publishing Manager (UK): Simon Pooley
Publishing Manager (SA): Thea Grobbelaar
DTP Cartographic Manager: Genené Hart
Editor: Melany McCallum
Design and DTP: Lellyn Creamer
Cartographer: Lucian Packies
Consultant: Rowland Mead
Proofreader: Thea Grobbelaar
Picture Researcher: Colleen Abrahams
Reproduction by Hirt & Carter (Pty) Ltd, Cape Town
Printed and bound in Hong Kong by Sing Cheong
Printing Co. Ltd.

Acknowledgements:
Christopher and Melanie Rice would like to thank Maria
Luisa Perestrello of the Regional Tourist Board in
Funchal for her assistance.

Cover Photographs
Top Left: *Farmers from across the island converge on
Funchal's Mercado dos Lavradores (Workers' Market).*
Top Right: *The pretty hamlet of Ponta do Sol is said to be
the sunniest spot on the island.* **Bottom Left:** *These
distinctive A-frame houses are typical of the Santana
region.* **Bottom Right:** *The Monte toboggan, a mode of
transport unique to Madeira.*

Title page: *Madeira's relaxed and carefree atmosphere
makes it the perfect place to unwind.*

CONTENTS

1
Introducing Madeira

Madeira is a Portuguese island dependency in the Atlantic Ocean, about 800km (497 miles) off the coast of Africa and 1000km (621 miles) southwest of Lisbon. On the same latitude as Bermuda, the mild subtropical climate is the stuff of legend, and was an important factor in attracting the first (mainly British) tourists at the beginning of the 19th century. Madeira is small – roughly the size of Menorca – but the sheer diversity of landscape and scenery is astonishing and greater than can be found in some countries. Towering volcanic peaks, dramatic gorges, great swathes of primeval laurel forest, river valleys clad in luxuriant vegetation, terraced hillsides planted with vines and bananas, cliffs of awesome dimensions – these are just some of the contrasts Madeira offers its visitors. Flowers of every description, introduced from Asia, Africa and the Americas or native to the island, appear in profusion and are without a doubt one of its prime assets. While Madeira is mostly mountainous, exploring the less accessible regions becomes easier (and more enjoyable) once you discover the *levada* trails that crisscross the rugged terrain.

Funchal is Madeira's capital and hub. Home to nearly half the inhabitants, it's a lively town with a beautiful coastal setting and there's enough in the way of historic buildings, parks, gardens and museums to occupy most visitors for at least a few days. Those seeking a more active holiday will relish the opportunities for golf, tennis, surfing, hang-gliding, scuba diving and sea fishing

ATLANTIC OCEAN

PORTUGAL

Oporto

LISBON

Spain

Strait of Gibraltar

Madeira

Morocco

TOP ATTRACTIONS

★★★ **Porto Santo:** the beach to beat all beaches – 9km (5.6 miles) of golden sand.
★★★ **Curral das Freiras:** spectacular valley, on every tourist itinerary.
★★★ **Pico do Arieiro:** Madeira's third highest mountain offers the best views.
★★★ **Monte:** toboggan rides, gardens and a cable car.
★★★ **Quinta do Palheiro Ferreiro:** plants and trees from Asia, Africa and America.
★★ **Cabo Girão:** the world's second highest cliff.
★★ **Adegas de São Francisco:** discover Madeiran wine.

Opposite: *Folk dancers in traditional costume pose for tourists.*

FACTS AND FIGURES

Population: Madeira
243,800; Porto Santo 4800.
The other islands are uninhabited. More than 40% of
the population lives in the
capital, Funchal. The population density on Madeira is
440 per km², one of the
greatest concentrations in
the European Union.
Government: Autonomous
Administrative Region within
the Republic of Portugal.
Language: Portuguese.
Religion: Roman Catholic.

in coastal resorts around the island. Madeira's unremit-
tingly rocky shoreline is an obvious drawback if you're
partial to lying out on sand; but with the beach at **Porto
Santo** only a ferry ride away, even this shortfall pales
into insignificance.

THE LAND

Madeira originated more than 20 million years ago from
a series of cataclysmic volcanic eruptions beneath the
Atlantic Ocean. Successive layers of rapidly cooling lava
and igneous rock built up from the seabed to raise a
cone-shaped island above the surface. In this respect,
Madeira resembles an immense iceberg: more than 60%
of its mass is hidden underwater, at depths of up to
3600m (11,800ft). Streams of molten ash and lava continued to flow down the sides of the cone, moulding the
ridge that forms the backbone of the island. This process
was completed some 1.8 million years ago. Madeira's
volcanoes were active for much longer, however – the
last eruptions occurred around 400,000 years ago, when
the magma flow created the caves of **São Vicente**.

Below: *The harbour at
Câmara de Lobos, with
Cabo Girão in the distance.*

Landscape

Madeira, then, is rugged and mountainous, nearly 50% of the terrain lying above 700m (2246ft). The highest point is **Pico Ruivo de Santana** at 1862m (6108ft). To the west of the mountain ridge is a deep, steep-sided ravine formed by the **Ribeira Brava** and the **Ribeira São Vicente** which effectively cuts the island in half, via the dramatic mountain pass at **Encumeada**. Beyond these river valleys is **Paúl da Serra**, a plateau of bleak, windswept moorland, 1400m (4593ft) above sea level. East of the central ridge the landscape becomes relatively less dramatic, as the peaks yield to gentler slopes and plateaus.

Above: *At 580m (1902ft), Cabo Girão is the world's second highest cliff.*

In the days of the discoverers Madeira was densely wooded and carpeted with thick vegetation. While much of the tree cover has disappeared, the valleys of the interior are still remarkably lush and hospitable, nowhere more so than **Rabaçal** with it laurel thickets, rampant ferns, cataracts and gorges. This rural idyll is a world away from the weather-worn headlands and gaunt, vertiginous cliffs of basalt and reddish tufa which make up the coastline. **Cabo Girão**, at 580m (1902ft), is the second highest cliff in the world. Five hundred years ago the first Portuguese settlers began cultivating the southern shoreline, which remains the most densely populated part of the island. Here every fragment of land is claimed for farming – the trademark *poios* (terraces), planted with vines, bananas, beans, maize, potatoes and other crops, a familiar feature of the Madeiran landscape.

Flora

When Madeira's first settlers set the forested island ablaze to clear land for farming, they unwittingly wiped out a priceless ecological inheritance. For this was no ordinary forest. The *laurissilva* (laurel forest), indigenous to the region, dated back to the Tertiary Era and had escaped extinction during the Ice Age, when the

---

GEOGRAPHY

Location: The Madeiran archipelago (Madeira, Porto Santo, Desertas and Selvagens) lies between latitude 32–33° north, and longtitude 16–17° west.
Area: Total surface area is 796km² (307 sq miles). Madeira is 57km (35 miles) long and 22km (14 miles) wide; Porto Santo is 11km (7 miles) long and 5km (3 miles) wide.
Highest peak: Pico Ruivo de Santana – 1862m (6105ft).
Highest cliff: Cabo Girão – 580m (1902ft).

FLOWERS IN BLOOM

• **January–March:** anemone, arum lily, camellia, camel's foot tree, cattleya, cymbidium, golden shower, mimosa, pride of Madeira, sword aloe.
• **April–June:** African flame tree, agapanthus, anemone, anthurium, camellia, cattleya, jacaranda, lupin, rhododendron, passion flower, star jasmine.
• **July–September:** agave, agapanthus, anthurium, belladonna lily, frangipani, golden trumpet, hydrangea, Madeiran orchid, Mexican dahlia, oleander, red hot poker, tears of Christ, tulip tree.
• **October–December:** belladonna lily, camellia, golden shower, golden trumpet, lady's slipper orchid, sword aloe, mimosa, poinsettia.
• **Year-round:** bougainvillea, hibiscus, honeysuckle, morning glory, strelitzia.

vegetation covering most of Europe was destroyed. Situated between 300m (984ft) and 1300m (4265ft) above sea level, the 15,000 or so hectares of laurel forest which has survived down to our own day was accorded UNESCO World Natural Heritage status in 1999 under the protection of the Madeira Nature Reserve. The forest contains a number of tree species, all members of the evergreen family, notably the *Lauris azorica* (bay tree), used locally in cooking, the *Vinhático*, better known as Madeiran mahogany, and the till (*Ocotea foetens*). The dragon tree (*Dracaeana draco*) deserves special mention. Famed for its reddish resin ('dragon's blood'), it is rarely encountered in the wild nowadays but its clusters of spear-like leaves are a familiar sight on Porto Santo.

Of the 200 floral species endemic to Macronesia (a region which includes the Canaries, the Azores and the Cape Verde islands), around 80 are indigenous to Madeira. Most of these grow on the uplands to altitudes of about 1000m (3280ft). They include the Madeira violet, the yellow foxglove, sow thistle and native species of geranium and orchid.

If Madeira deserves the epithet 'floating garden', much of the credit must go to the British, keen amateur gardeners who exploited to the full the mild climatic conditions and rich volcanic soil. The manifests of British

merchant vessels calling at Funchal read like a horticul-
turist's wish list of bulbs and seeds, collected from the
remotest corners of the globe. Two centuries on and the
legacy is plain for all to see in the towering camellia trees
with their brilliant white and red-streaked flowers, the
araucaria pines from Brazil, the cedars from the Atlas
Mountains, the South African proteas and pink-flowered
amaryllis, the Australian banksias, Japanese wisteria and
Mexican frangipani. And the cornucopia is not confined
to rural *quintas* and public gardens. Jacaranda trees flourish beside Funchal's traffic-clogged roads, bougainvillea
cling to the river embankments, while the alluring fra-
grance of jasmine escapes the bounds of garden walls.

Bird Life

While Madeira lies some way off the main migration
route and attracts a relatively small variety of breeding
birds, it still holds plenty of interest, not only for trained
ornithologists but for keen amateur bird-watchers. The
Desertas and Selvagen islands, both remote and uninhabited, are officially protected sanctuaries for sea birds like
shearwaters and petrels. Closer to home, Fea's petrel has
been spotted off Porto Santo, while Cory's shearwater
sometimes makes an appearance off the coast of Madeira
itself – especially around Ponta de São Lourenço. Balçoes
is another bird-watching
'hot spot', as are the São
Jorge estuary (occasional
sightings of the greylag
goose here), Palheiro
Ferreiro golf course
(swifts, grey herons, rock
doves, etc.), and the coastline between Funchal and
Cabo Girão (kestrels,
buzzards and lesser black-
backed gulls). Ruddy
turnstones and the occa-
sional sparrowhawk have
also been seen around

USEFUL WEBSITES

Search engine for sites on
Madeira: **www.
madeiraonline.com**
Official tourist board site:
www.madeiratourism.org
Turivema, specialists in
walking tours: **www.
madeira-levada-walks.com**
Company specializing in
mountain bike hire, canyoning, jeep safari, jet ski rental,
trekking, etc.: **www.
madeira-island.com/
aventura**
Books, cakes, wine, CDs, etc.:
**www.madeira-shopping.
com**

Opposite: *Distinctive
A-frame houses are typical
of the Santana region.*
Below: *Strelitzias and
proteas thrive in the semi-
tropical Madeira climate.*

DAYS OF THE WEEK

If you're looking to check the opening and closing times of a restaurant, bar, theatre, etc., it might help to know the days of the week in Portuguese, which differ from the French, Italian or Spanish pattern. They are:
Domingo: Sunday
Segunda-feira: Monday
Terça-feira: Tuesday
Quarta-feira: Wednesday
Quinta-feira: Thursday
Sexta-feira: Friday
Sábado: Saturday

Funchal harbour. Near the water's edge, keep an eye out for the oystercatcher, the little egret (a type of heron), and periodic visitors like the grey wagtail (actually mainly yellow). Two bird species are endemic to Madeira: the long-toed pigeon (*Columba trocaz*) and the Freira – the laurel forest is their natural habitat. The canary – indigenous to Macronesia – is commonplace while Berthelot's pipit, a small warbler with greyish-brown, almost tawny, feathers, has been spotted in numbers around Ponta de São Lourenço. Also look out for endemic subspecies, including the yellow-legged gull, the blackcap (a small warbler attracted to shrubs, even in the gardens of Funchal), the firecrest (another warbler with a distinctive red and gold head stripe, preferring a woodland habitat), and the chaffinch. Porto Santo is the breeding ground of the hoopoe. Its highly distinctive colouring (fawn, with startling black and white bars on wings and tail) makes it easy to identify. If you're looking for a memento of your visit, ask about the stamp series *Madeiran Birds*, issued by the Portuguese post office.

Climate

Madeira is renowned for its mild, subtropical climate: average annual temperatures of around 22°C (72°F) in summer, usually falling no lower than 16°C (61°F) in winter. The Gulf Stream ensures that sea temperatures too are invitingly warm, ranging from a low of 17°C (63°F) in March to a high of 23°C (73°F) in September. What complicates the picture is the effect of microclimates on weather patterns. As any regular visitor will confirm, the Paúl da Serra may be shrouded in freezing mist, while Funchal

Below: *Typical Madeiran landscape – nearly half the island lies above 700m (2246ft).*

basks in warm sunshine. Generally speaking, the south coast is the hottest part of the island, particularly the Bay of Funchal that is sheltered by a ridge of mountains to the rear. On the sunniest days, the temperature can climb to 27°C (81°F) or even higher. The humidity too is more tolerable here, thanks to cooling onshore breezes. Nevertheless, the capital is not immune to the effects of the *capacete* (peaked cap or helmet), a bank of cloud which blankets the coast from late morning to mid-afternoon when it retreats to the mountains. This phenomenon (irritating to sunbathers) is most pronounced in February, March and June. If you're looking for uninterrupted sunshine, your best bet is Porto Santo. Much less bearable than the *capacete* is the *leste*, a searing easterly originating in the North African desert which can send temperatures rocketing to 40°C (104°F) for a few days each summer, when humidity levels sink to 13% or even lower. At this time the air fills with a fine, reddish, Saharan dust. By contrast, the average temperature on the north coast is around 1.5°C lower than, the south, while humidity is up to 10% higher. Further inland, the mountainous areas are cloudy for much of the year, to an altitude of around 1200m (3937ft). Above that level, however, visibility is usually excellent.

Many visitors to Madeira are surprised by the amount of rainfall. Generally speaking, windy, rainy days are more frequently encountered on the exposed northern coast than in the south. For

Above: *Tropical fruits make a colourful display in a Funchal market.*

FRUITS IN SEASON

Custard apples: January–April.
Strawberries: March–June.
Cherries, apricots: May, June.
Pawpaw, figs: June–October.
Plums: June, July.
Grapes, melons:
  August–October.
Mangoes, avocados:
  September–December.
Grapefruit: September–
  November.
Pears, apples: October–
  March.
Oranges: November–March.
Bananas: year-round.

FUNCHAL	J	F	M	A	M	J	J	A	S	O	N	D
MIN TEMP. °C	13	13	13	14	16	17	19	19	19	18	16	14
MAX TEMP. °C	19	18	19	19	21	22	24	24	24	23	22	19
MIN TEMP. °F	56	56	56	58	60	63	66	67	67	65	61	58
MAX TEMP. °F	66	65	66	67	69	72	75	76	76	74	71	67
HOURS OF SUN DAILY	5	6	6	7	7	7	8	8	8	7	5	5
RAINFALL mm	64	74	79	33	18	5	0	0	25	76	89	84
RAINFALL in.	2.5	2.9	3.1	1.3	0.7	0.2	0.0	0.0	1.0	3.0	3.5	3.3
DAYS OF RAINFALL	6.0	6.0	7.0	4.0	2.0	0.9	0.2	0.4	3.0	7.0	6.0	7.0

Above: *Following a* levada *trail is one of the most enjoyable ways of seeing Madeira.*

example, while precipitation in Funchal averages 550mm (22 inches) per annum, it is nearly four times higher in the north, thanks to cyclonic Atlantic fronts which deposit the rainfall on the slopes of the forested hinterland. Even in the capital, however, some rain can be expected from October to May, usually in the form of short but violent cloudbursts. Again, Porto Santo is the ideal refuge for anyone averse to rainfall.

Levadas

Unlike the Canary Islands or Porto Santo, Madeira is blessed with a super-abundant water supply. One scientist has estimated that the hidden reserves amount to a staggering 8 billion cubic metres, enough to last not only the present millenium but many more to come. The problem is that, while the south of the island enjoys most of the sunshine and is potentially more fertile, most of the rainfall is concentrated in the north. The early Portuguese settlers wasted little time in coming up with a solution – a system of narrow watercourses channelling rain and spring water directly to the fruit orchards and sugar plantations along the south coast. Today these *levadas* (from the Portuguese *levar*, 'to carry') crisscross the island, covering a distance of more than 2150km (1335 miles). No mean feat, when you consider that the labourers used only chisels and pickaxes and risked life and limb cutting their way into the sheer rock, sometimes suspended in hanging baskets over steep precipices, or crawling on their hands and knees through tunnels hewn in the mountainside.

The *levadas* are administered directly by the Madeiran government, which charges farmers and market gardeners for the service by the 'flow hour'. Day-to-day management is in the hands of the *levadeiro* who is responsible for operating the sluice gates (water is channelled to the farms following a pre-arranged timetable), for repairing fire or storm damage and for clearing away

---

THE REAL COLUMBUS?

During the 1980s an entertaining, if far-fetched, thesis was put forward that the discoverer of America was not an Italian born in Genoa in 1451 but a Portuguese, born in the Alentejo three years earlier. Even more sensational was the claim that Christopher Columbus was really Salvador Fernandes Zarco, illegitimate son of the Duke of Beja, grandson of the discoverer of Madeira, João Gonçalves Zarco, and great-nephew of Henry the Navigator. The story goes that he adopted the name Columbus in 1485 on the orders of King João II – part of his cover as a member of the Portuguese secret service. His task? To convince the King and Queen of the viability of a *western* sea route to the Indies, leaving the Portuguese navigators, Bartholomeu Dias and Vasco da Gama, to open up the eastern route via the Cape of Good Hope!

leaves and other debris. Pathways, designed originally for the convenience of the *levadeiro*, have become an important source of income for the island's burgeoning tourist industry, as visitors come to realize that *levada* walking is one of the more exhilarating ways of appreciating the diversity of Madeira's landscape.

HISTORY IN BRIEF

According to the Portuguese chronicler, Gomes de Azurara, the Madeiran archipelago was discovered by chance. In 1418 two naval commanders, João Gonçalves Zarco and Tristão Vaz Teixeira, were exploring the west coast of Africa when they were blown off course during a storm and washed ashore on Porto Santo. When they returned to Sagres, their base in the Algarve, they reported having seen a much larger island to the south, shrouded in mist. The Portuguese heir to the throne, the Infante Enrique (better known as Henry the Navigator), ordered them back to investigate and, in 1420, they found their mystery island which Zarco christened Madeira, 'the wooded isle'. In fact, the discovery of Madeira is unlikely to have been an accident. All the islands in the archipelago had been charted by the end of the 14th century and the Medici Atlas, compiled by Genoese cartographers in 1351, even refers to Madeira as the 'wooded island' (Isola de Lolegname in Italian dialect). It seems unlikely then that Henry the Navigator, the founder of a School of Seamanship, would have been unaware of their existence. In any event, Madeira and Porto Santo were officially declared Portuguese territory in 1425 and handed over to Henry's captains to administer. João Gonçalves, nicknamed Zarco ('one-eyed') after losing an eye at the Siege

Below: *Traditional azulejos (painted tiles) add to the appeal of the Monte Palace Tropical Garden.*

MALMSEY

In England, Malvasia wine is also known as malmsey. In 1478 the nobleman, George Duke of Clarence, was despatched to the Tower of London on a charge of high treason. Told to prepare for death, he was invited (so it is said) to choose a means of execution and asked to be drowned in a butt (vat) of malmsey. In Shakespeare's *Richard III*, the duke is stabbed first: 'Take that, and that; if all this will not do, I'll drown you in the malmsey-butt within'. According to the bard, malmsey was also the favourite tipple of Sir John Falstaff (*see Henry IV Part 2*).

of Ceuta (Morocco), was assigned the west of the island and governed from Funchal, while his companion, Teixeira, took charge of the east from his base at Machico. The Italian adventurer, Bartolomeu Perestrelo, who had joined them on their second voyage, oversaw the settlement of Porto Santo. The arrangement seems to have worked well.

The Early Settlers

Colonization began almost immediately. First on the scene were the scions of the Portuguese nobility who formed the island's landowning elite. Their names – Freitas, Bettencourt, Almeida, etc. – live on to this day through their innumerable descendants. There were also distinguished exiles: Sir John Drummond, a refugee from the Scottish court, for example, and a former king of Poland, known locally as Enrique Alemão. More crucial to the development of the island's economy were the entrepreneurs and merchant-financiers from Italy, Spain and northern Europe (especially the Flemish ports of Bruges and Antwerp). Artisans and labourers from mainland Portugal provided the workforce until the first contingent of slaves arrived from the Canary Islands in 1452.

For Zarco, clearing the dense virgin forest for cultivation was a priority. Great swathes were set alight and left to burn out of control for weeks, even months on end – seven years, according to one chronicler! Today's environmentalists would not have approved of the wholesale destruction, but the tree ash did add to the fertility of the volcanic soil. To stimulate agriculture, the fields and clearings were leased to members of the aristocracy for a specified period, during which they were

CRISTOVÃO COLOMBO

expected to make improvements on the land that would eventually be theirs. This incentive scheme seems to have paid off. Grain and other cereals were grown for subsistence, while the first vine terraces were planted on the hillsides of the southern coast. The extremely lucrative trade in sugar ('white gold') began in the 1470s and peaked in 1506. Christopher Columbus was just one of a galaxy of foreign merchants who profited from the export of this precious commodity to markets across

Opposite: *Christopher Columbus married a daughter of Bartolomeu Perestrelo, one of the founders of Madeira.*

HISTORICAL CALENDAR

20mBC Madeira is formed from spectacular volcanic eruptions beneath the surface of the Atlantic Ocean.

1.7mBC As the volcanoes cool, a distinctive Madeiran landscape begins to take shape.

AD77 There is a reference to Madeira in Pliny the Younger's *Natural History*.

1351 A Genoese map identifies three islands off the African coast. Madeira is named the 'Wooded Isle' (Isola de Lolegname).

1418 The naval commanders, João Gonçalves Zarco and Tristão Vaz Teixeira, step ashore on Porto Santo for the first time.

1419–20 The Portuguese colonization of Porto Santo and Madeira begins with the blessing of Prince Henry the Navigator.

1425 Madeira is officially declared a province of Portugal.

1452 The first slaves arrive on Madeira from the Canary Islands. They work the sugar plantations and begin building a network of irrigation channels (*levadas*).

1478 The explorer, Christopher Columbus, then a sugar merchant, visits Funchal on business, before marrying the daughter of the governor of Porto Santo.

1514 According to the island's first census, the population is 5000, excluding slaves.

1566 The French adventurer, Bernard de Montluc, sacks Funchal and massacres the garrison (250 men).

1580–1640 Madeira is ruled from Spain after Philip II claims the Portuguese crown.

1662 The marriage of Charles II of England to Catherine of Braganza, daughter of João IV of Portugal, boosts trade with Madeira.

1703 The Methuen Treaty further encourages British merchants to settle on Madeira. Soon the wine trade is almost exclusively in their hands.

1768 The British navigator and explorer, Captain Cook, calls at Madeira on his first voyage in the *Endeavour*.

1801–02 First British occupation of the island during the Napoleonic Wars.

1807–14 Second British occupation. Many of the 2000 garrison choose to stay on and settle.

1846 Potato crop fails.

1851 The fungus *Oidium tuckeri* attacks the vines, devastating the crop.

1856 A cholera epidemic kills around 10,000 inhabitants.

1891 Reid's Hotel opens, stimulating tourism.

1916 Germany declares war on Portugal and Funchal is shelled by U-boats.

1931 A general strike is declared on Madeira following a banking collapse and a sudden rise in bread prices. An attempted coup d'état is put down by the Portuguese army.

1939–45 World War II. Portugal remains neutral, but Reid's Hotel closes and refugees from Gibraltar take shelter on the island.

1964 The opening of Santa Catarina airport ends the long isolation of the island.

1974 Democracy is restored in Portugal after a bloodless military coup.

1976 Madeira is granted special status as an autonomous region within Portugal.

1986 Portugal enters the EU, bringing increased investment to the island.

1997 Via Rápida motorway opens, cutting the journey time from Funchal to Ribeira Brava from one hour to 15 minutes.

2002 The redevelopment and expansion of Funchal airport is completed with expected benefits for the tourist industry.

Above: *Madeira has been producing quality wines since the 16th century.*
Opposite: *This shrine to the Virgin Mary at Terreiro da Luta was erected in the 1920s.*

SLAVES AND SUGAR

Portuguese historians have recently challenged the commonly held assumption that Madeira's sugar plantations were worked exclusively by slaves. Records for the parish of Calheta (a major sugar-producing area) show that just 7% of the island's slaves were resident there. In fact the highest concentration of slaves was in Funchal, not a major sugar-producing area. Labour on the plantations was mixed, free men working alongside slaves for wages or payment in kind. The Madeiran sugar industry could have survived without any slave involvement at all.

Europe. These entrepreneurs dominated banking, commerce and shipping on the island and had a controlling interest in the timber yards. Conducting their business outside the Customs House in Funchal, they were immediately recognizable by their fashionable dress and ostentatious behaviour. Some married into the Portuguese nobility, while many bought land and eventually settled down on the island – men like Giovanni Lomelino, whose descendants built Quinta das Cruzes, Simone Acciaiuoli, a noted collector of Flemish art, and Jennin d'Esmerandt, one of Madeira's most powerful plantation owners and friend of Columbus. By 1508, Funchal had a population in excess of 5000 and was Portugal's third city after Lisbon and Porto. It owed much of its prosperity to the slave workforce, which now numbered around 3000: Guanches from the Canary Islands worked alongside Berbers from North Africa, Guineans and men and women from the Portuguese East Indies. It was these human chattels who built the sugar mills, laboured on the plantations and constructed the first *levadas*.

From Sugar to Wine

Sometime the bubble had to burst. Over-production, soil exhaustion, the increasing cost of slaves and, most importantly, competition from Brazil slowly eroded Madeira's lead in the sugar trade. Demand began falling in the first decade of the 16th century, but the islanders were quick to find an alternative source of revenue. Within 50 years most of the plantations had become vineyards. The nascent industry flourished thanks largely to the introduction of the Malvasia grape from the Greek islands – visitors to Madeira, like the Venetian navigator Alvise de Mosto, commented on the quality of the wine being produced. Among the more innovative cultivators were the Jesuits, who opened a college on the island in 1572. The quality of the Malvasia from their vineyards at Quinta Grande (west of Cabo Girão) and Fajã dos Padres was legendary and they are usually credited with introducing new varieties like Bual and Sercial. While the Spanish occupation of Portugal from 1580–1640 had a negative impact on sales – the Spanish were keen to promote their own wines – by the mid-17th century, Madeira was exporting 12,000 barrels annually, to the American colonies, the West Indies and Europe.

For the islanders, the only fly in the ointment was the very real threat of pirate attack. Porto Santo was particularly vulnerable to raids by corsairs from the Barbary Coast. In 1617 Algerian sailors wreaked havoc on the population, massacring most of the men and taking the women and children captive. The psychological scars remained with the survivors, who left Porto Santo for good, taking refuge in the hills of Santo da Serra. On the mainland the worst incident took place in 1566 when a French adventurer, Bertrand de Montluc, attacked Funchal, wiping out the garrison before unleashing his force of 1000 men on the beleaguered inhabitants.

The British Connection

England and Portugal sealed what was to become the longest political association in history in 1386, when King João I married Philippa of Lancaster, the future mother of Henry the Navigator. British interest in Madeira, however, was slower to develop. Trading concessions granted by

> ### MADEIRA – THE US CONNECTION
>
> From 1668 only Madeiran wines were allowed into Britain's American colonies and within 50 years the American market accounted for around 25% of total sales. A genuine liking for Madeira soon developed, so much so that in 1768 a riot broke out in Boston Harbour when British customs officials tried to impound a consignment of smuggled wine – a dress rehearsal for the famous tea party five years later. Madeira was used to toast the Declaration of Independence in 1776 and to mark the inauguration of George Washington as first US president in 1789. The drink remained fashionable throughout the 19th century but never recovered from the impact of the Prohibition. There are still aficionados in Georgia, however, where the Madeira Club of Savannah holds regular meetings.

POISON PEN

One visitor's impressions were not published in her lifetime. The Englishwoman, Isabella de França, spent her honeymoon on Madeira in 1853 – her husband was the son of a local merchant. The newlyweds, aged 58 and 50 respectively, threw themselves into the social round, Isabella later confiding her frequently acerbic thoughts to her diary, which she illustrated herself. *Journal of a Visit to Madeira and Portugal* was finally published in 1969. The original forms part of the collection of the **Casa Museu Frederico de Freitas** in Funchal. (It was Dr Freitas who discovered the manuscript in the 1930s, gathering dust in a local bookshop.)

King João IV in 1654 were renewed following the marriage between Charles II of England and the Portuguese princess, Catherine of Braganza, in 1662. Shortly afterwards Madeira was exempted from protectionist measures aimed at boosting British exports at the expense of the Dutch, their long-standing rivals on the high seas. This gave Madeira's British merchants a virtual trading monopoly with the American colonies as well as the West Indies. Their business interests were further consolidated by the Methuen Treaty of 1703 which dramatically reduced the import duty paid on Madeiran wines entering England.

While the merchants lived lives of unashamed luxury on their *quintas* and vineyards, ordinary Madeirans fared less well. Effectively the island's economy had been transformed into a monoculture dependent on wine (up to 70% of cereals were now imported). Crop failures, a fall in wine prices, or a dramatic shift in the political climate (the American War of Independence for, example) were harbingers of famine and destitution for the poorest sections of the population. Unemployment, low wages and other social ills were laid at the door of the British, who were often perceived as arrogant or condescending. The precarious nature of the Madeiran economy was even more keenly felt as the population continued to rise, from around 50,000 in 1754 to 84,000 half a century later.

Opposite: *A decorative feature in the tropical gardens of Quinta das Cruzes, Funchal.*
Right: *Colourful fresco by the German artist, Max Romer, in the Adegas de São Francisco, Funchal.*

When British interests in Madeira were threatened during the Napoleonic Wars, the immediate response was to occupy the island – not once, but twice (1801–02 and 1807–14). A rash of intermarriages (not to mention less formal sexual liaisons) was one consequence, and when the garrison finally disbanded, many soldiers chose to stay on, among them the future wine merchant, John Blandy. Madeira was to witness the final act of the Napoleonic era when, in August 1815, *HMS Northumberland*, en route to St Helena with the banished former emperor on board, dropped anchor in Funchal harbour. The British consul, Henry Veitch, visited the ship and provoked a minor diplomatic incident by addressing Bonaparte as his majesty, a faux pas which eventually led to his dismissal.

The Birth of Tourism

Just off the Avenida do Infante in Funchal visitors can still see the beautiful grounds of the **Hospício da Princesa**. The hospice for sufferers of tuberculosis was founded by the Empress of Brazil in memory of her daughter, Maria Amélia, who died of the disease in 1853 at the age of 22. The unfortunate young woman was one of thousands of invalids who came to Madeira hoping that its famously mild winter climate, recommended by doctors throughout Europe, would improve their health. By the end of the 19th century there were even guidebooks written specifically for patients, for example the Marquis degli Albizzi's *Madère: Guide practique pour malades et touristes*. Travelling with the

FOREIGN AID

The economic crisis of the 1840s and 1850s was so grave that the governor of Madeira twice appealed to the international community for relief. The contributing countries included Great Britain, the United States, Germany, Russia and Ireland – this at the time of the potato famine. On a visit to Madeira in 1849 the Dean of Ely commented that 'not even in the worst parts of Ireland' had he seen 'more intense misery than among the people of this island'.

Right: *Fish hanging out to dry on the waterfront of Câmara de Lobos.*

NAPOLEON'S MADEIRA

During his famous stay in 1950, Sir Winston Churchill gave a dinner for the British community in Reid's Hotel. As a special treat he served his guests bottles of 1792 vintage Madeira, regaling them with the story of how the British consul, Henry Veitch, presented Napoleon with a consignment of this finely aged wine on his way to exile in 1815. This intriguing anecdote seems to have originated with one of Madeira's great characters, Dr Michael Grabham, who owned the wine in the 1930s. Cold water has since been poured on the story by Alex Liddell in his book *Madeira* (Faber, 1998). Liddell points out that, as this particular wine was not bottled until 1840, it could hardly have been offered to Napoleon, who died 20 years earlier. According to Grabham's son, Walter, Grabham senior had a tendency to 'embroider some of his statements.'

invalids were their physicians, nurses and companions who whiled away the time writing letters, keeping diaries, sketching, painting or compiling travelogues. Some of their output (mainly engravings and water-colours of the exotic flora, fauna and scenery) is exhibited in the **Quinta das Cruzes Museum** and offers a fascinating insight into the early travellers' perception of the island. When they returned home, the more colourful accounts appeared in magazines like the *Illustrated London News*, fanning interest. While the voyage from Liverpool to Funchal still took around 13 days, the number of visitors was increasing at a remarkable rate, so much so that by the middle of the 19th century Madeira's income from tourism was estimated at around £40,000 a year. Not only the sick, but colonial civil servants on leave from India and the Far East, clergymen, vacationing businessmen and their spouses, journalists, artists, botanists and geologists all found much to wonder at. Visiting royalty brought an extra cachet to the island. Following Prince Adalbert of Prussia came Queen Adelaide (widow of William IV of England), Princess Maria Carlotta of Saxony, Archduke Maximilian von Habsburg and the Empress Elizabeth of Austria. For the British, who formed by far the largest contingent, Funchal soon became a home-from-home with its English church, croquet lawns, tea gardens, cricket and football matches, not to mention Consul Veitch's notorious 'Madeira parties'. Also *de rigueur* was to sit for a portrait at Senhor Vicente's photographic studio, which opened in 1865 to cater for the growing demand for holiday souvenirs.

Hard Times

Few contemporary travelogues make mention of the series of disasters of near Biblical proportions which visited the island around mid-century. First, in 1846, the potato crop failed. Then, in 1851, a fungus, *Oidium tuckeri*, began attacking the vines with such devastating effect that many experts wrote off the industry altogether. While the islanders were still reeling under these blows, cholera struck, killing around 10,000 men, women and children – 10% of the population. Finally, the vine louse, *Phylloxera*, decimated the wine harvests of 1872–82. Thousands of agricultural workers were reduced to begging on the streets as the government launched not one, but a succession of appeals for international aid. For many, however, the response was too little too late, leaving emigration as the only way out. By 1910 more than 80,000 men, women and children had vacated the island for good, creating a Madeiran diaspora in Brazil, Guyana, Angola and South Africa. They are remembered today in the Monument to the Madeiran Emigrant on Funchal's waterfront.

The Twentieth Century

The new century began with a crisis of a different kind. In 1905, the German government approached the Portuguese with proposals for an ambitious development programme for the island. On reading the small print, Lisbon discovered that the plans

JUMPING FLEA

The *braguinha* (see page 26) takes its name from the northern Portuguese town of Braga where it was originally known as the *cavaquinho*. Madeiran emigrants hoping to start a new life in Hawaii towards the end of the 19th century brought the unusual four-stringed instrument with them. It was an immediate hit with the Pacific islanders, who were so impressed by the performers' deftness of touch that they re-christened the *braguinha* 'jumping flea' (ukulele). One of the more enterprising Madeiran families – Nunes by name – began marketing a more compact version of the instrument that was patented in the United States in 1917. The ukulele's heyday was the 1920s when it featured in numerous minstrel shows and Vaudeville turns.

Below: *Madeira's recently expanded Santa Catarina airport is only a short drive from Funchal.*

included not only the building of new hospitals and sanatoria as originally promised, but a string of luxury hotels and even a casino (gambling was illegal at that time). The British suspected (not without reason) that what was actually envisaged was a commercial takeover of the island, and persuaded the Portuguese to renege on the agreement. Relations between the Germans and the Portuguese soured as a consequence, and deteriorated further when German property on Madeira was confiscated on the outbreak of World War I. In December 1916 Funchal was lightly shelled following a U-boat attack on Allied shipping but, apart from a similar incident the following year, the island emerged from the conflict relatively unscathed. The damage to the economy, however (both wine exports and tourism), was considerable.

In the postwar period, Portugal's political instability mirrored the situation elsewhere in Europe. A military coup in 1924 brought a hitherto obscure economics professor, Dr Antonio Salazar, to prominence. By 1933 Salazar was effectively a dictator, retaining power until his death in 1968. The consequences for Madeira were felt even before Salazar was securely in the saddle. In 1931 his stringent financial policy led to a sudden hike in bread prices and a banking collapse which, at a stroke, wiped out many of the islanders' savings. A general strike was declared, supported by several hundred recently exiled political prisoners. Lisbon despatched troops to quell the unrest but some defected,

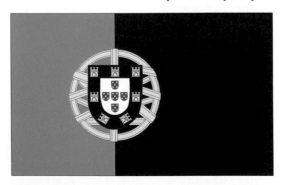

leading to an attempted coup by rebel general Sousa Dias. The Portuguese eventually put down the uprising but not before panic set in among the British residents, many of whom fled the island. Others sought shelter in Reid's Hotel, which was picketed by a small force of British troops.

Economically speaking, Madeira remained the poor relation throughout the Salazar dictatorship until his successor was overthrown in a bloodless coup, known as the 'Carnation Revolution', in 1974. The restoration of democracy was followed two years later by the introduction of a new constitution, which gave Madeira a greater degree of autonomy than it had ever previously enjoyed.

GOVERNMENT AND ECONOMY

The Portuguese constitution of 1976 designates the Madeiran archipelago an Autonomous Political Region. The people of the island elect a head of state, the President, along with the 50 members of the parliament or Legislative Assembly. This body is responsible for all matters of direct concern to the island, including taxation, customs duties and public services. Madeirans also elect five deputies to the Portuguese parliament. The government in Lisbon oversees foreign policy and defence, and has the final say in all constitutional issues. Portugal's representative on the island, the Minister of the Republic, has a residence in Funchal. The Madeiran President appoints a cabinet comprising a vice president and six secretaries of state. Local government is in the hands of elected town councils.

For more than a quarter of a century, power has been in the hands of the Popular Social Democratic Party (PSD), which won the first elections (1976) by a landslide, with around 65% of the vote. The PSD was last reelected in October 2000. Their leader, the charismatic Dr Alberto João Jardim, became president in 1978 and is still in office.

Above: *A monument to João Gonçalves Zarco (see panel page 34) by the island's most famous artist, Francisco Franco. It was unveiled in 1934 and won the praise of the Portuguese dictator, Dr Salazar.*

Opposite: *Madeira is a dependency of Portugal.*

Right: *Bananas account for nearly half the island's total exports.*
Opposite: *Fishermen play cards to while away the idle hours.*

Madeira and the European Union

The mainstays of the Madeiran economy are farming, viticulture, fishing, handicrafts (mainly embroidery and wickerwork), tourism, and offshore financial services. Agriculture still employs more than one fifth (21%) of the workforce. The most important single crop is bananas, accounting for 45% of the island's total exports. Tourism is an increasingly visible source of revenue, the majority of visitors coming from Portugal, Britain and Western Europe, including Scandinavia. While unemployment has fallen to around 4% (a much lower figure than on the mainland), the Madeiran GDP per capita is only 30% of the European average and less than 60% of the average Portuguese.

Impressive levels of economic growth have been achieved (albeit from a very low base) since Portugal joined the European Union in 1986. Two decades of political stability have undoubtedly helped, but the unprecedented rise in the living standards of most Madeirans during the 1990s would have been inconceivable without massive EU funding. During 1990–93 alone, the Community contributed US$ 370m to developing the island's infrastructure, and by 2005 the Regional Development Fund and other European agencies will be providing close on 80% of total investment. To date, most of the money has been spent on road construction, schools, hospitals and vocational training. The most ambitious single project, the redevelopment of Funchal airport, cost upwards of US$ 455m. Another EU initiative, the creation of a Free Trade Zone around the port of Caniçal (severely affected by the international ban on whaling in the early 1980s), has had mixed results. While more than 5000 new jobs have been created on the 29.6ha (73.1-acre) site (mainly in manufacturing and light industry), the generous tax incentives, subsidies and fiscal exemptions have not attracted the anticipated levels of private investment.

THE PEOPLE

The majority of Madeirans are of Portuguese origin, descendants of settlers from the Algarve and Alentejo who began colonizing the island in the 15th century. Portuguese is the official language and mother tongue of Madeirans, though English is spoken by a growing number of young people and is widely used in business. The population figure of 243,800 does not include the diaspora of around one million expatriate Madeirans, living in countries as far apart as Venezuela and South Africa. Emigration has been a significant demographic factor since the middle of the 19th century, though the trend has recently been reversed. Not all the returning migrant families are welcomed with open arms. While they bring investment and entrepreneurial skills, their relative prosperity and extravagant lifestyle are the underlying causes of resentment.

Madeira remains a deeply conservative society committed to the traditional values of home and family. The Roman

> **HERITAGE**
>
> One of the most active Madeiran communities abroad hails from **New Bedford** on the eastern seaboard of the United States. It was towards the end of the 18th century that American whalers began calling at **Caniçal** to enlist experienced crews for expeditions out in the Atlantic. More often than not, the final destination was New Bedford, where many Madeiran sailors eventually chose to settle. The Club Madeirense SS Sacramento is dedicated to preserving Madeiran customs and traditions and, with the active support of President Jardim, has recently financed the Museum of Madeiran Heritage. New Bedford also has its own home-grown folk band, the Grupo Folkloric Madeirense.

Catholic Church, which claims the allegiance of around
97% of the population, exercises a powerful influence in
this respect. However, there are growing signs of change
as a younger generation, increasingly educated outside
the island and finding work in the towns rather than the
countryside, questions the old mode of thinking.

The Traditional Way of Life

To discover how Madeirans observe their time-honoured
customs and traditions, check out a typical village **festival** *(festa)*. These lively celebrations usually mark the
feast day of the local saint or one of the red-letter days in
the agricultural calendar (the grape or chestnut harvest,
for example). Some festivals are associated with a local
legend or miraculous event – the crucifix recovered from
the sea near Machico, for instance. The procession to the
church of Our Lady of Monte which takes place on the
Feast of the Assumption (15 August) is the most solemn
of these occasions and
attracts pilgrims from all
over the island.

Folk music is another
Madeiran tradition worth
investigating, though nowadays it's the exclusive
preserve of bands and
choirs, performing in hotels
or established venues like
the Café Relógio in
Camacha. Well-known
names who have recorded
on CD include the Grupo
Folclórico da Camacha,
Banda d'Alem and
Encontros da Eira. Songs
like *Cerfeiras* (The
Harvesters) and *Baile do
paspalhao* (Dance of the
Lark) relate to life in the
fields. *Na Noite do pão*

(Night of the Bread) was traditionally sung on Christmas Eve by women baking bread for the following day's festivities. Crafts too had their own tunes, the embroiderers' *Si Que Brade*, for example. Songs of Moorish origin include the *Cantiga do preto* (Black Man's Song), characterized by a monotonous drum beat, and the *Carrier's Dance*, in which the performers imitate the ponderous movements of men and women carrying heavy loads, their feet weighed down by chains. In a lighter vein, the dance of the *Camacheiras* features a young couple who stop to argue on the way to a feast, until they're enveloped by other merry-makers and their quarrel is forgotten. All dancers wear the standard Madeiran folk costume of white shirts and baggy trousers (men) or white blouse with red embroidered cape and waistcoat and long, multicoloured striped skirt (women). Men and women wear the *carapuca*, a skullcap with a twirled point. They perform to the accompaniment of the *rajão* or *braguinha* (both relatives of the mandolin), the *raspadeiro* (a notched stick played like a washboard), *castanholes* (castanets) and the *briquinho*, rings of cloth puppets which dance and jangle as the stick to which they are attached is pounded on the ground.

Above: *Plaintive strains of* fado *music emanate from the restaurants of Funchal's Old Quarter.*
Opposite: *Folk troupes perform for tourists during major festivals.*

Embroidery

The art of embroidery (*bordados*) arrived on Madeira with the discoverers – in those days it was more or less the exclusive preserve of Portuguese noblewomen. Some of the oldest surviving examples, created by the nuns of the Santa Clara Convent in Funchal, are now on display in the Museu de Arte Sacra. The cottage industry that

---

FADO

Fado (the word means 'fate') is to the Portuguese what Flamenco is to the Spanish. Plaintive and dramatic, the songs (usually ballads) tell of lost or unrequited love and the vicissitudes of life: 'soul' music, one might say. *Fado* is said to have originated in the drinking dens of Lisbon, and may have African or Arab roots. Accompaniment is usually provided by the guitar. One of the best places to hear authentic *fado* (if a little touristy) is Arsénio's in Funchal's old town.

brought the beauty and complexity of Madeiran embroidery to the notice of the world is of more recent origin and was the initiative of an Englishwoman, Elizabeth Phelps. The daughter of a highly respected wine merchant and philanthropist, she taught needlework at an orphanage in Santana. Her fascination with traditional Madeiran embroidery led her to take samples to England, where they caused a minor sensation at the Great Exhibition of 1851 in London. Almost overnight Madeiran embroidery came into vogue, especially for wedding gowns – so much so that demand outstripped supply until a British firm set the business on a more commercial footing in 1862. More than 1000 jobs were created, an unexpected boon for the many women whose husbands were out of work following the crisis in the vineyards. When the fashion eventually ran its course around 1900, a German entrepreneur, Otto von Streit, came to the rescue with the labour-saving technique of printing the designs directly onto the fabric. This revolutionized the business and by the 1920s, around 70,000 women were employed in the craft. Today the figure is closer to 10,000, but embroidery still outstrips wine in terms of exports.

The seamstresses, known as *bordadeiras*, work from home, their skills passed within families from one generation to the next. The materials – cotton, linen, natural silk and organdie – and the patterns are supplied by agents working on a commission basis. Usually two or three women work on one item, each specializing in a particular stitch or design embellishment. The finishing touches are added at the 'factory' where the embroideries are washed and ironed before receiving the official seal of authenticity from IBTAM (*see* page 51). Italy, Germany, France and the United Kingdom are the most important export markets. Despite a good showing at the Lisbon World Exhibition in 1998, Madeiran embroiderers are finding it increasingly difficult to compete with China and the Far East, where labour costs are lower and marketing more aggressive.

Food

Madeiran cooking differs little from that of mainland Portugal; however, there are one or two pleasant surprises in the way of regional specialities – the scabbard fish (*espada*) for example. No one visiting the fish market in Funchal will forget the serrated teeth and repellent, almost insolent stare of this creature of the deep. But the white flesh is both tender and succulent and goes down a treat with the traditional side dish of bananas fried in butter. Parrot fish (*bodião*), tuna (*atum*), sea bream (*pargo*), hake (*pescada*) and mackerel (*carapau*) are the supporting cast. *Bacalhau* (salted cod, shredded and fried with onions, egg, garlic and potatoes) and *cataplana* (a seafood casserole of clams, prawns, squid and white fish, cooked with herbs and accompanied by a generous helping of rice) are imports from mainland

Opposite: *Wickerwork is an important cottage industry in Camacha.*
Below: *One of Madeira's most popular dishes is* espada *(scabbard fish), usually served fried, as here, with bananas, or in wine and garlic.*

apple • *maçã*
baked • *no forno*
beer • *cerveja*
bill • *conta*
boiled • *cozido*
bottle • *garrafa*
bread • *pão*
breakfast • *pequeno almoço*
butter • *manteiga*
dinner • *jantar*
drinks • *bebidas*
eggs • *ovos*
fish • *peixe*
French fries • *friesbatatas fritas*
fried • *frito*
garlic • *alho*
glass • *copo*
grilled • *grelhado*
lemon • *limão*
lunch • *almoço*
meat • *carne*
menu • *ementa*
orange • *laranja*
pepper • *pimento*
red wine • *vinho tinto*
rice • *arroz*
roasted • *asado*
salt • *sal*
shellfish • *mariscos*
stewed • *estufado*
table • *mesa*
tourist menu/fixed-price •
  menu turistical de preço fixo
white wine • *vinho branco*

Portugal. If you're looking for a fish starter, try limpets (*lapas*), served in their shells in a pool of garlic butter. Of the meat dishes, the most typically Madeiran is *espetada* – skewered chunks of prime beef, rubbed in salt and garlic, garnished with a bay leaf and (to be properly authentic) grilled over a charcoal fire kindled with laurel twigs. *Espetada* is an essential constituent of any village festival, a reminder that, until comparatively recently, meat was reserved for special occasions. Some former staples of the Madeiran diet still appear as side dishes – *milho frito* (fried cornmeal), for example, and *pão de batata* (brown bread made with sweet potatoes). Beans (another mainstay of the farm workers' diet) feature prominently in *feijoada* (a nourishing soup almost thick enough to qualify as a casserole). If you're fond of soups, look out for *açorda*, made of bread flavoured with garlic and olive oil and with a poached egg as the *coup de grâce*. Desserts are usually an 'also ran' in this part of the world, although one can hardly complain when the fresh fruit on offer might include anything from mangoes and passion fruit to strawberries, figs and bananas. You may also be offered Madeiran cheesecake (*queijadas da Madeira*) or *bolo de mel*, a dark cake made with honey, molasses, almonds and dried fruit, seasoned with cloves.

Right: *Seafood is in plentiful supply in Madeira's restaurants.*

Drink

Madeiran fortified wine is widely available in restaurants. The drier varieties (Sercial and Verdelho) are generally recommended as apéritifs and should be served chilled (though not ice cold). The smoother Bual goes well with dessert, while Malvasia (Malmsey), the sweetest, should be deferred until coffee. The Portuguese wine, *vinho verde* ('green' referring not to the colour but to the youthfulness), is preferable to the locally produced wine, which rates only as *vinho da casa*. Beer drinkers may find *Coral* lager, brewed on Madeira since the 19th century, to their taste. Imported beers are not widely available and are of course much pricier. As a refreshing alternative to beer try the local cider, distilled in the southern valleys around Santo da Serra. Liqueurs are something of a Madeiran speciality – the choice includes *ginga* (made with cherries), *castanha* (chestnuts), or *amêndoa* (almonds). *Poncha*, made with sugar cane, lemon juice, honey and brandy, should be handled with care! If you don't enjoy alcohol, look out for the refreshing passion fruit drink, *brisa maracujá*.

Above: *Beer has been brewed on the island since the 19th century.*

COFFEE LOVERS

The Portuguese are enthusiastic coffee-drinkers and there are numerous ways of saying how you want your coffee served. Ask for *um café* and you'll be given a regular black coffee. If you need something stronger, go for *uma bica*, the closest thing to espresso. Some Madeirans though will prefer it weak (*uma carioca*). Coffee with milk is *café com leite*, but for a really milky coffee you'll want *um galão* (served in a glass). Finally, in the hot summer weather, iced coffee (*café gelado*) goes down a treat.

2
Funchal

The Madeiran capital enjoys a superb setting: a sweeping bay crowned by a diadem of mountain peaks. (The advantages of the natural harbour must have been obvious to the captain discoverers.) The name Funchal derives from *funcho*, the Portuguese for fennel – it's said that Zarco discovered large quantities of this aromatic plant growing on the banks of local rivers. As one Madeiran in two now lives here, it's no surprise that the town corners the lion's share of the tourist trade, most visitors spending at least a few days in the capital before moving on to tour the rest of the island. For sightseeing purposes, Funchal is relatively compact and can be comfortably explored on foot. Most things worth seeing can be found in the narrow streets around the 16th-century cathedral (**Sé**) and the **Convento de Santa Clara**. A stroll along the seafront brings two other historic buildings into view: the **Old Customs House** (now the regional parliament) and the **Palácio São Lourenço**, once the cornerstone of the city's defences. Shopping starts with the famous covered market (**Mercado dos Lavradores**) or the souvenir shops on Avenida Zarco. The best area for eating out, in the evenings especially, is the **Zona Velha** (Old Town), where you can enjoy the twin culinary favourites, *espada* (scabbard fish) and *espetada* (beef or chicken kebab), while listening to *fado*, the Portuguese equivalent of the 'blues'. The **Hotel Zone** at the opposite end of the town has its own bars, restaurants and nightlife, including a casino.

ATLANTIC OCEAN

Madeira

Santa Cruz

FUNCHAL

Don't Miss

*** Jardim Botânico: subtropical flora in a magnificent setting.
*** Adegas de São Francisco: wine lodge famous for its Madeira.
*** Sé: the cathedral, one of the oldest buildings on the island.
** Quinta das Cruzes: traditional Madeiran villa in beautiful grounds.
** Museu de Arte Sacra: religious art in the former Bishop's Palace.
** Zona Velha: Funchal's old quarter – bars, restaurants and traditional *fado* music.

Opposite: *The hillsides around Funchal harbour offer spectacular views.*

JOÃO GONÇALVES ZARCO

Surprisingly little is known about the founder of Madeira. He was born in Portugal in 1395 but whether in Santarém (northeast of Lisbon), Tomar or Matosinhos, a coastal village north of Porto, is still a matter of debate. On entering the service of Henry the Navigator, Zarco played a prominent role in the Siege of Ceuta in 1415 but lost an eye in the process. Shortly afterwards, according to the Portuguese chronicler, Diogo Gomes, Zarco clashed with Castilian sailors while exploring the coast of West Africa, and it may even have been a Castilian defector who encouraged him to set his sights on **Porto Santo**. Zarco's tenancy of Madeira lasted almost 50 years. At some point during the 1450s, he built a house on the site of what is now **Quinta das Cruzes**. When he died, at the grand old age of 80, he was buried in the **Convent of St Clare** in Funchal.

It's possible to see a good deal of the island using Funchal as a base. A cable car now takes visitors up to **Monte**, while the inland beauty spots of **Curral das Freiras** and **Boca da Encumeada** are accessible by car. Alternatively there are boat trips exploring the southern coast, from **Cabo Girão** in one direction to **Ponta de São Lourenço** in the other.

TOWN CENTRE
Convento de Santa Clara

Halfway up Calçada de Santa Clara you'll spot the entrance to one of the oldest religious foundations on the island. The Convent of St Clare was founded in 1496 by Zarco's grandson, João Gonçalves de Câmara; his sister, Dona Isabel, was the first abbess. Only the island's wealthiest families sent their daughters here and they expected a spiritual return on their investment. Not all the young ladies went willingly – this was an enclosed order, after all, and the commitment was for life. Happily, today's sisters are all volunteers. You can visit the church on your own but to tour the convent you'll need a guide (allow about 45 minutes). If you have no Portuguese, the sister will make a bold stab at French or English, more likely a mixture of the two! There's no charge but a small donation is appreciated.

Right: *The cloisters in the Convent of Santa Clara are the oldest part of the building.*

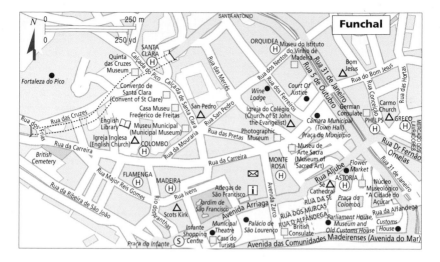

The cloistered garden occupies the oldest part of the building, though there's no longer any trace of the chapel built by Zarco in the 15th century. What you'll see instead are faded little shrines decorated with gilded stucco and glazed *azulejo* tiles – note the camellia motifs. The convent's treasures, a motley collection of reliquaries, gilt altars, polychrome statues and framed portraits of the saints, date mostly from the 17th and 18th centuries. There's a fine view of the harbour from the windows on the first floor. You're shown the dormitories and the choir, where an iron grille in the wall allows the nuns to follow mass in the church below from the seclusion of the convent.

Only a single Gothic arch has survived from the original 15th-century church, but the 17th-century successor is a gem in its own right. Looking up, you might be standing inside a huge casket inlaid with yellow, blue and green *azulejos*, the painted timber ceiling forming the lid. João Gonçalves Zarco, the discoverer of Madeira, is buried under the high altar where the sanctuary lamps always remain lit. The convent is open daily from 09:00–12:00 and from 15:00–18:00 (ring the bell).

NUN'S STORY

The story of one of the 19th-century novices reads like the romantic plot from a Donizetti opera. Maria Clementina, a young woman renowned for her beauty, was browbeaten into entering the convent by her parents, who were unwilling to provide her with a dowry. Just two years later, however, fate came to the rescue when Portugal's new secularist government banned enclosed orders from keeping nuns against their will. Still only 20 years old, Maria promptly fell in love with a handsome army officer. But before they could tie the knot, another change of regime forced her back inside the gates where she languished until her death in 1850, aged 46.

Above: *A coat of arms in the gardens of Quinta das Cruzes.*

Quinta das Cruzes **

A little way up the hill from the Santa Clara convent, on Calçada do Pico, Quinta das Cruzes is the archetypal Madeiran manor house. If, as is alleged, Zarco built a house here in the 15th century, precious little of it has survived. In the 17th century the estate belonged to the Lomelino family, Genoese wine merchants still commemorated in the chapel. Today's 19th-century mansion has been refurbished from assorted private collections and is open as a museum. The furnishings include handsome Regency consoles, and chairs designed by the famous English cabinet-makers, Thomas Chippendale and George Hepplewhite, but probably manufactured on the island. The indigenous craftsmen showed greater ingenuity converting packing cases used for storing sugar into beautifully fashioned cupboards and boxes. If you're not bowled over by furniture and silverware, there's Sèvres porcelain, Delft pottery, enamel from Limoges, Chinese vases and Portuguese crib figures to admire. The 19th-century lithographs and watercolours reflect a contemporary fascination with the native flora and fauna, not to mention the scenery, of this dazzling island.

Step into the garden to enjoy the floral firework display: hibiscus and bougainvillea, fuchsias and azaleas, dragon trees and Indian laurels, mimosa, eucalyptus, Norfolk Island pines and palm varieties indigenous to Mexico, Malaysia and Colorado. The scattered archaeological remains include a couple of Manueline window frames and what's left of the *pelhourino* – the Funchal pillory. Open Tuesday–Saturday 10:00–12:30 and 14:00–17:30; Sundays 10:00–13:00.

Igreja Inglesa

Tucked away on Rua do Quebra Costas, the English Church is easily missed but worth tracking down. A sedate and seemly reminder of the British presence on the island, it was completed in 1822 to a design by the multi-talented Henry Veitch. The neoclassical style, much in vogue at the time, was also in step with Portuguese law – Protestant churches were not to resemble (or compete with) their Roman Catholic counterparts. Bells were specifically outlawed! During the 1840s the community was torn apart by a bitter sectarian dispute between High and Low Church members of the congregation. The row scandalized Queen Victoria and ultimately led to the founding of a rival chapel. In the garden you'll see a bust of Philippa of Lancaster, the mother of one of Portugal's great maritime heroes, Henry the Navigator. The library is also open to visitors.

Before the **British Cemetery** was founded in 1765 non-Catholics were buried at sea. The move to the present site on Rue da Carreira took place in 1887 – scenically an inspired choice. Read the epitaphs on the mossy headstones and you'll be reminded of the poor souls who arrived on the island already invalids, many of them victims of tuberculosis (*see* panel, page 87). Open daily from dawn to dusk.

Below: *Unusually on Madeira, the English Church was built in the neoclassical style.*

CASA DOS AZULEJOS

Dr Freitas' collection of *azulejos* is exhibited in the recently opened wing alongside the Casa Calçada in the **Museu Freitas**. Apart from hand-painted tiles, you can see mosaics from the Convento de Santa Clara and an accompanying video (in Portuguese only) explaining the art and history of *azulejo* production. There is also a museum café selling tea, coffee and light refreshments.

Casa Museu Frederico de Freitas

Turn onto Calçada de Santa Clara and keep an eye out for the **Casa de Calçada**, the town house with the red perimeter wall, opposite the church of São Pedro. Frederico Cunha de Freitas, a lawyer whose lifelong passion was collecting, lived in this 18th-century mansion for many years and on his death left his entire estate, including his priceless collection of antiques, curios and *objets d'art*, to the people of Madeira.

At a first glance, it's hard to believe Dr Freitas found time for anything *but* collecting. The hand-painted *azulejos*, of Persian, Turkish and *Mudéjar* design, date from the 13th–19th centuries and form one of the finest collections of their kind in the world. Religious sculptures from the Portuguese East Indies, paintings, prints and engravings, woodcarvings, antique furniture, porcelain and ceramics (an amazing 2000 milk jugs, teapots and vases) – everything on display reflects the lifelong passion of one extraordinary individual and his travels around the world. Open Tuesday–Saturday 10:00–12:30 and 14:00–18:00, tel: 291 220 578.

Museu Municipal

The municipal museum, at rua da Mouraria 31, is devoted solely to natural history. This part of Funchal was

Below: *Museu Freitas, with the church of São Pedro in the background.*

once inhabited by Berber slaves from North Africa (Mouraria refers to Moors). The museum was originally the private residence of the Count of Carvahal; it's still known as the **Palácio São Pedro** and is worth seeing in its own right. Most visitors, especially those with children in tow, make a beeline for the **Aquarium**, where the main attractions are the native eels and *garupas*. The natural history collection dates back to the 1850s and, unless you happen to be a vacationing taxidermist, the stuffed sea birds, fossilized corals and nuggets of volcanic rock are unlikely to set the imagination on fire. Yet it was the patient cataloguing of the island's flora and fauna by local naturalists that paved the way for today's nature reserves and national parks. Open Tuesday–Friday 10:00–18:00, Saturday–Sunday 12:00–18:00, tel: 291 229 761.

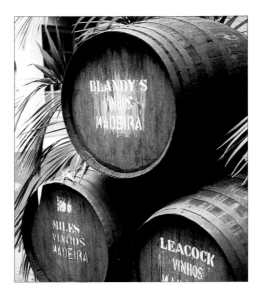

Above: *English families have a long association with Madeira wine.*

Adegas de São Francisco ***

The wine lodge on Avenida Arriaga, no. 28, is now the headquarters of the **Madeira Wine Co.** and a showcase for the island's best-known export. The buildings date from the 17th century and originally belonged to a Franciscan convent (hence the name); in the 1840s they were acquired by the Blandy family. John Blandy, a quartermaster with the British garrison during the Napoleonic Wars, arrived on the island in 1807 and started the family wine business four years later.

The rambling lodge, its whitewashed walls and timber ceilings reeking of old wines, is one of Madeira's top attractions, with more than 200,000 visitors a year. The tour begins in the reception area where you'll see murals by German artist Max Romer celebrating the

---

SLAVES AND MASTERS

The largest concentration of slaves was in the parishes of Sé (Cathedral) and São Pedro. The majority were indentured not to plantation owners but to noblemen and members of the clergy. They undertook a wide variety of tasks, working in the fields or as clerical assistants, artisans or domestic servants. Women also sold farm produce in the local markets. Unlike the situation on the plantations of the New World, slaves were not purchased in large numbers. One of Madeira's most conspicuous landlords, João Esmeraldo, owned only 14 slaves.

Above: *A view of Funchal's harbour district from the hotel zone.*

ESTUFALGEM

The discovery that *estufalgem* improved Madeiran wines happened quite by accident. It was well known that wine deteriorated in the course of long voyages unless it was fortified with alcohol distilled from cane sugar. But it was not until the second half of the 17th century that connoisseurs noted a marked improvement in wines that had made the long round trip to India. At the time this was attributed to the pitching and tossing motion of the ships, but it was later realized that the warm weather en route was responsible. Wines that had undergone such voyages were promoted as 'round trip' wines (*vinhos de roda*). By the end of the 19th century most producers had switched to the time saving *estufalgem* process of artificial heating in warming rooms or tanks.

---

wine harvest. Through the rustic-looking cobbled courtyard is a covered passageway that was originally a medieval street running down to the harbour. The guide reveals some of the arcane mysteries of the wine-making process. After harvesting, the crop is taken to Funchal for fermentation, a process that takes from four to six weeks. The next stage is known as *estufalgem* (*see* panel). The wine is matured in 'warming rooms' or in stainless-steel tanks, heated to a temperature of around 45°C (113°F) and left for at least three months. (Vintage wines, known as *vinhos de canteiro*, are still warmed naturally by the sun's rays.) Each consignment or 'lot' is then left for about two years to 'rest' in oak casks before blending. It's usually at this stage that the wine is fortified with brandy until it reaches an alcohol level of 18–20%.

In the museum you'll see some of the paraphernalia associated with the trade: rough-hewn presses, barrels of formidable girth made from oak or Brazilian satinwood, goatskin wine carriers, hoop irons, etc.

After the tour, there's a short film on the history of wine making and the Blandy connection. Then comes the visit to the tasting rooms and an opportunity to buy. Madeira improves with age – Vintage wine must mature in the cask for a minimum of 20 years and Extra Reserve for 15. It's also extremely durable as professional tasters, allowed the privilege of sampling bottles over 150 years old, eagerly testify. Malvasia (Malmsey) and Verdelho are sweet wines which go well with coffee and dessert. Bual (medium dry) is an excellent complement to soups; while the dry, lightly scented Sercial (which should be served chilled) makes the perfect apéritif. The lodge is open for guided tours only: Monday–Friday 10:30 and 15:00, Saturday 11:00, tel: 291 740 110.

HARBOUR DISTRICT

The long arm of the **Molhe da Pontinha** (harbour wall) incorporates the old fort of **Nossa Senhora da Conceição**. Gone are the days when rowing boats sailed out to meet the incoming ships anchored off Loo Rock, while young boys dived for coins tossed to them by visitors waiting to be escorted into port. Today, Funchal mainly handles container traffic, although you will see the occasional liner, not to mention the Porto Santo ferry (daily sailings from the new quay, *cais nova*). For a 15th-century navigator's eye view, take a trip on the *Santa Maria*, a faithful replica of Columbus's ship, which makes part of the 90-minute journey under sail, weather permitting. Helicopters also take off from the harbour on sightseeing tours (tel: 291 232 882).

Spread out on the higher ground behind the port are the gentle slopes of the **Parque de Santa Catarina**. A romantic spot for an evening's stroll as the sun sets over the bay, the landscaped gardens are also a good place to bring children. Apart from the play area, there are benches for picnic stops and you can watch the swans glide effortlessly across the lake or luxuriate in the semi-tropical flora. The gardens are named after a wooden

> ### DEEP-SEA FISHING
>
> The fishing season begins in mid-June and continues until early October, weather permitting. During that period boats leave regularly from Funchal Marina in search of bonito, amberjack, dolphin-fish and other species. The best sport, however, is provided by the blue marlin. These streamlined creatures of the deep are a challenge to any hook-and-reel fisherman, being elusive, smart and fast, attaining speeds of up to 45kph (28mph). The female blue marlin is also extremely powerful and can weigh up to 900kg (2000 pounds) – more than six times the average male.

Harbour District

Visitors to **Parque de Santa Catarina** will notice a statue commemorating two Portuguese aviators, Gago Coutinho and Sacadura Cabral. The two naval officers made the first air crossing from Lisbon to Madeira in March 1921. This pioneering journey was a test run for the maiden transatlantic flight from Lisbon to Rio de Janeiro the following year. Flying a Rolls-Royce-powered Fairey flying boat and using a revolutionary new sextant developed by Coutinho himself, the duo set off on 30 March 1922 and were in sight of the Brazilian coast when they were forced to ditch after running out of fuel. The Portuguese navy despatched another flying boat and the intrepid pair resumed their odyssey, but were again forced to ditch. They eventually arrived in Rio on 17 June, piloting their third aircraft.

Below: *The 15th-century Chapel of St Catherine was founded by Zarco's wife.*

chapel built on the orders of Zarco's wife, Constança Rodriguez, in 1425. Today's building is a charming 17th-century impostor – only the diminutive bell tower and the water font, decorated with scenes from the life of St Catherine, survive from the Manueline era.

Any roundup of the park's attractions would have to include **Quinta Vigia**, the pink mansion by the lake, now the official residence of the Madeiran president; the sub-tropical gardens of the **Casino Park Hotel** (designed by the architect of Brasilia, Oscar Niemeyer), and *The Sower*, an arresting scupture by Francisco Franco.

On the other side of Avenida do Infante is the **Hospício de Princesa**. Now a school, this was originally a sanatorium for patients suffering from tuberculosis. It was founded by the Empress of Brazil to commemorate her daughter, Maria Amélia, who died of the disease in 1853. The dragon trees are the outstanding feature of the gardens.

Avenida Arriaga

The main artery into town from the **hotel zone** links the **Sé** (Cathedral) with the **Parque de Santa Catarina**. Leaving Funchal, on the corner of Avenida Zarco you'll see a bronze statue of João Gonçalves Zarco, the founding father of Madeira, by Francisco Franco. On your left, opposite the tourist office and the Adegas de São Francisco, are the fortified walls of the **Palácio de São Lourenço**. The keystone of Funchal's defences, São Lourenço was founded early in the 16th century and was still under construction when French corsairs descended on the town in 1566, seizing the fort and massacring the defenders. Refurbished in the 18th century as a palace, São Lourenço's military significance remains – today this is the residence of the military commander (closed to the public except for pre-booked guided tours – contact the tourist office). Opposite the **Jardim de São Francisco**, the Toyota car showroom hardly deserves its elegant premises. The colonial-style building, formerly the **trade halls of the Chamber of Commerce**, is decorated with blue and white *azulejos* from the 1920s, depicting scenes from local life including the Monte toboggan run.

Funchal's exquisite **Municipal Theatre** (Teatro Baltasar Dias) dates from 1888. It's an important venue for plays and other cultural events, including concerts by the Madeira classical orchestra and a folk music festival at the end of October. If you get the chance it's definitely worth a look inside to see the gilded private boxes and the beautiful painted ceiling, complete with rubicund cherubs, or *putti*. At the roundabout just before Avenida do Infante is another statue by Francisco Franco, this time commemorating the explorer king, **Henry the Navigator**.

Above: *The most attractive car showroom in the world?*

TAMING FUNCHAL'S RIVERS

Funchal's rivers were once formidable waterways, prone to flooding when swollen by heavy rainfall. In 1803 all three rivers burst their banks with devastating effect: more than 600 people were killed, while dozens of houses and other buildings were destroyed. In the wake of the disaster, a Portuguese military engineer, named Reginald Oudinot, was called in to make the rivers safe. The stone embankments built by his sappers did the trick and survive to this day.

Above: *Founded in the 16th century, the fortress-palace of São Lourenço still has its own military commander.*

Avenida das Comunidades Madeirenses (Avenida do Mar)

The official name for the esplanade stretching from the **Parque de Santa Catarina** to the **Zona Velha** has proved a bit of a mouthful even for the locals; it's more commonly known as Avenida do Mar. This is the perfect spot for a stroll, before dinner or late on a warm summer night when the main distraction, apart from the rhythmic murmur of the sea, is the souvenir stalls, specializing in cheap novelties (miniature bicycles ingeniously fashioned out of twisted wire, etc.) If, like most people, you've left your present-buying to the last minute, you'll find plenty of ideas at the **Casa do Turista**, a showcase for traditional Madeiran handicrafts: embroidery, wickerwork, pottery, glassware and so on.

The marina is a more obvious landmark. From here there are boat excursions to Ribeira Brava in one direction, and Ponta de São Lourenço and Caniçal in the other. Moored alongside the marina you'll notice **The Beatles Restaurant** among the flotilla of floating eateries. (Once upon a time the yacht was the plaything of the legendary pop group.) On the landward side, beyond manicured lawns and fountains, is the immaculate façade of the **Palácio São Lourenço**. The **Old Customs House** on Rua de Alfândega predates it by some years; sadly, few of the original Manueline features have survived the successive restorations. Today the Customs House is the headquarters of the regional parliament. Funchal's rivers, now tamed and prettified by trailing bougainvillea, are relatively inconspicuous but you'll spot two of them carving their way through the town from a point near the end of the avenue.

Núcleo Museológico 'A Cidade do Açúcar'

Given the importance of 'white gold' in Madeira's history, a museum devoted to the sugar trade is only to be expected. But the site on Praça do Colombo is famous for another reason. The original 15th-century house (demolished in the 1870s) belonged to a wealthy Flemish sugar merchant named Jennin Esmerandt. One of Esmerandt's friends, it turns out, was none other than Christopher Columbus, who stayed here on at least one occasion. The foundations of Esmerandt's house were excavated in 1989 to reveal the remains of an old cistern. Other finds open a window onto life at the time, not only the coins, buttons, fragments of porcelain, metal weights, beads, goats' teeth and rats' bones, but the remnants of food (nuts, cherry stones, grape seeds, a shredded pineapple kernel) – each tells its own story. In the adjoining room you'll see maps, charts and artefacts connected with the sugar trade, including the distinctive conical moulds which feature on Funchal's coat of arms to this day. Open Monday–Friday 10:00–12:30 and 14:00–18:00, tel: 291 236 910.

FESTIVAL ROUND-UP

The most important village festivals are mentioned in the text. The following is a summary. All the events below take place in Funchal unless otherwise indicated.

• **January:** New Year firework display is among the most spectacular in Europe.
• **February:** Rio-inspired Carnival procession and fancy dress parade with music and dancing into the small hours.
• **April:** Flower Festival (*see* panel page 48).
• **June:** *Fins de Semana Musicais* (Musical Weekends). Concerts of classical music featuring top Madeiran performers.
• **August:** Feast of the Assumption (15 August). Religious festival celebrated all over the island but especially in Monte.
• **September:** Grape Harvest. Bacchanalian revels in Funchal, also villages across the island.
• **December:** Christmas. Highlights include street illuminations (using three-quarters of a million light bulbs) and crib displays.

Left: *Children play an important role in Funchal's annual carnival procession.*

HORSE RIDING

Horse riding opportunities are limited, but do exist: **The Riding Association**, open Tuesdays–Sundays, offers rides at an hourly rate with individual tuition geared to experience. Contact **Associação Hípica da Madeira**, Quinta Vale Pires Caminho dos Pretos, São Gonçalo, Funchal, tel: 291 792 582 or 291 792 910. The **Quinta S. Jorge**, owned by Crowne Plaza, enjoys a picturesque location near Santo da Serra. The riding school offers lessons at an hourly rate and excursions through the wooded countryside with magnificent views of the Atlantic. Contact: **Crowne Plaza**, Estrada Monumental, 175–177, Funchal, tel: 291 717 700, fax: 291 717 701. On the east of the island, contact **Quinta do Pâtano**, Casais Próximos, Santo da Serra, Machico, tel: 291 552 577, fax: 291 552 071.

Sé ★★★

Funchal Cathedral on Largo da Sé dates from the same period as the Old Customs House and the Santa Clara Convent. It was completed in 1514 under the patronage of Manuel I, whose reign coincided with the discovery of the Americas, earning him the soubriquet 'fortunate'. The cathedral is an early example of Manueline architecture, a uniquely Portuguese blend of Gothic and Renaissance styles, characterized among other things by exuberant sculptural decoration – the sailor's knot motif on the pinnacles of the east end is a typical ornamental embellishment. The architect, Pêr Annes, hailed from the Alentejo in southern Portugal where Moorish influences were still strong; this explains other decorative touches like the *azulejo* tiles on the spire. The simple, almost minimalist, façade is more in keeping with a village church than a cathedral – only the coat of arms of King Manuel above the portal hints at the building's status. The interior also holds a surprise or two. Allow your eyes time to adjust to the gloom, then gaze upward at the carved ceiling, among the finest in Portugal. Fashioned from native cedar wood and overlaid with ivory, the mesmerizing geometric patterns are a typical Arab device. As you stroll down the nave towards the apse, you'll be amazed by the painted arabesques on the vaults, as engaging as the tangled

borders of an illuminated manuscript. The paintings on the gilded reredos are by 17th-century Portuguese artists. Don't leave without taking a closer look at the carvings in the choir stalls. The work of 17th-century Flemish craftsmen, they're a witty commentary on urban life of the period with nattily dressed merchants standing in for the apostles. Open daily 09:00–12:30 and 16:00–17:30, tel: 291 228 156.

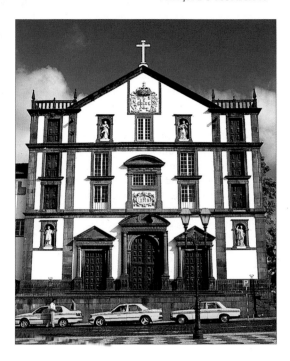

Left: *Founded by the Jesuits, the Igreja do Colégio overlooks Funchal's main square, Praça do Municipio.* **Opposite:** *Manueline doorway on the façade of Funchal Cathedral.*

PRAÇA DO MUNICIPIO

There are several reasons for making a short detour to Funchal's busy main square. If you haven't done so already, this is your chance to visit the **Museu de Arte Sacra**. Alternatively, cross the square's wavy mosaic floor to the **Igreja do Colégio**, otherwise known as the Church of St John the Evangelist. Designed by a Portuguese architect, Bras Fernandes, it was completed in 1629, almost 60 years after members of the Jesuit Order first arrived on Madeira. The statues on the austere Baroque façade are of St Ignatius Loyola, St Francis Xavier, St Stanislaus and St Francis Borgia, four outstanding figures in the Order. The church is open only for services; if you get the chance, take a look at the retable behind the high altar – the woodcarvings, overlaid with gold leaf, are reckoned to be among the finest in Portugal. The adjacent buildings are now part of the University of Madeira.

BOAT EXCURSIONS

Taking a boat trip is both enjoyable in itself and an excellent and energy-saving way of exploring the Madeiran coastline. Most of the companies listed below operate from Funchal Marina. Destinations include Ribeira Brava, Ponta do Sol and Baia de Abra (near Prainha). **Moser** organizes a 5 hour tour of Porto Santo with swimming stops (May to October only).

Albatroz Organization: Marina do Funchal, tel: 963 003 864.

Costa do Sol: Marina do Funchal, tel: 291 224 390, fax: 291 235 735.

Santa Maria, Actividades Marítimo-Turísticas: Marina do Funchal, tel/fax: 291 220 327.

Aquanautica Gavião: Caminho do Avista Navios 4, Funchal, tel: 919 911 293, fax: 291 772 030.

URS Moser Boat Trip: rua João Gonçalves Zarco 5, Porto Santo, tel/fax: 291 982 162.

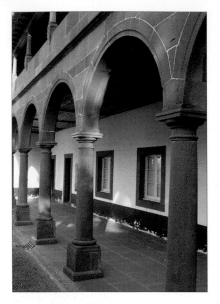

Funchal's handsome town hall (**Câmara Municipal**) is on the opposite side of the square. The original owner was a Portuguese nobleman, who commissioned it as his private residence in 1758. The exquisite marble statue of Leda and her swan in the courtyard is more appealing than the lacklustre local history museum upstairs.

Museu de Arte Sacra **

The Museum of Sacred Art, on the corner of Rua do Bispo and Praço do Municipio, is a cultural treat which should not be missed. Of the original Bishop's Palace, completed around 1600, only the chapel and the covered balcony facing the square (best viewed from the window between floors) survived the earthquake of 1748; the Baroque reconstruction was completed nine years later. The exhibition is spread over two floors and can be viewed comfortably in a couple of hours. The collection of embroidered vestments and liturgical silverware, assembled from religious foundations across Madeira, is remarkable given the size of the island. Look out for the gold-plated processional cross, presented to the chapter of Funchal Cathedral by King Manuel I (1495–1521). The Portuguese paintings date from the 16th–18th centuries. Several of Madeira's founding families were artistic patrons; Grão Vasco's splendid *Adoration of the Magi*, for example, was financed by a prominent member of the Teixeira clan, while the descendants of Zarco himself crop up in the panels of a triptych ostensibly commemorating SS James and Philip. The majority of Madeira's patrons, though, were sharp-eyed merchants who had amassed huge fortunes from the sugar trade and were looking to build new reputations for themselves as men of taste – the Italian, Simon Acciaiuoli, for example, who appears with his wife in a *Descent from the Cross*. The museum's small

FLOWER FESTIVAL

A colourful event in the Madeiran calendar, the Flower Festival takes place over two days in April or early May. The children's costume procession launches the weekend's celebrations that culminate in the building of a floral 'wall of hope' (*muro de esperança*) in the **Praça do Municipio**. The street parade held the next day showcases Madeira's flora and handicrafts. The procession starts at the **Parque de Santa Catarina** and follows **Avenida Arriaga**, ending in the Largo do Colégio (details from tourist information). Prime vantage points, such as the balcony of the Golden Gate Restaurant, are snapped up weeks in advance.

but remarkable collection of Flemish art is founded on works now reliably attributed to Dirk Bouts, Gerard David, Jan Provost and Joost van Cleve, painters of repute who have earned a place in the world's leading galleries. Open Tuesday–Saturday 10:00–12:30 and 14:30–17:30, Sunday 10:00–13:00, tel: 291 228 900.

Museu do Instituto do Vinho de Madeira

Not far from the Praça do Municipio, on Rua 5 de Outubro (no. 78) you'll see an imposing building with a tall watchtower. It's the headquarters of the Madeira Wine Institute, the ultimate authority responsible for all aspects of production and quality control. Those precious bottles of Sercial or Verdelho you've bought as presents for friends – or for you own consumption – will already have received the *selo de garantia* (seal of authentication) from the institute. A small but engaging museum traces the history of wine production on the island, mainly through photographs, prints and engravings, although you'll also see examples of wine presses and barrel-making equipment (a cooper is occasionally on hand to demonstrate the craft). The explanations are thorough and will appeal particularly to wine buffs.

Appropriately enough, the building was formerly the home of wine merchant, Henry Veitch. He designed it himself and it became the prototype for colonial residences in India, South Africa and Mozambique. Open Monday– Friday 09:00–12:30 and 14:00– 17:00, tel: 291 220 581.

Opposite: Originally the bishop's palace, the Museu de Arte Sacra has a distinguished art collection. **Below:** *Bougainvilleas contribute to Madeira's colourful floral displays by flowering throughout the year.*

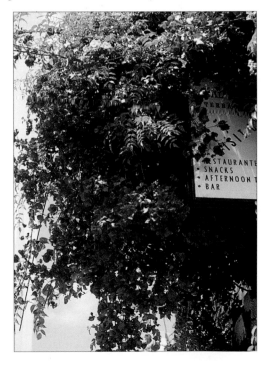

MARITIMIO FOOTBALL

Funchal's highly successful football team plays at the **Estádio dos Barreiros** (Barreoros Stadium), Rua do Dr Pita, tel: 291 223 747. Most games take place on Sunday afternoons or week-day evenings. Tickets are sold at the ground on match days and at other times from the club museum or shop (rua Dom Carlos I, 14).

Mercado dos Lavradores

Funchal's indoor produce market is on Rua Dr Fernão Ornelas on the edge of the **Zona Velha**. It was built in the early 1940s in the regional style known as 'Novo Estado' and with the customary *azulejo* decoration. The best time to visit is on Friday or Saturday when farmers from the furthest reaches of Madeira trundle into town with truckloads of fruit and vegetables. Enjoy listening to the banter and soak up the colours – the flower sellers are here in force, wearing their distinctive candy-striped skirts and red waistcoats. So are the island's fishermen with their catches of tuna, scabbard and shellfish. If you're shopping for a picnic, look out for the small, sweet bananas – Madeira is one of only two native pro-ducers within the EU (the Canaries is the other). If you've worked up an appetite, there are snack bars *in situ*, or you can head for one of the cafés in the Old District. Open Monday–Thursday 07:00–16:00, Friday 07:00–20:00, Saturday 07:00–15:00, closed Sunday.

ZONA VELHA **

Below: *Farmers from across the island converge on Funchal's Mercado dos Lavradores (Workers' Market).*

Funchal's 'Old Quarter' lies to the east of the modern town and dates back to the early 16th century. At that time it was known as 'Santa Maria' after a church which no longer exists but is still commemorated in the street name, **Rua de Santa Maria**. For a long time this was a run-down part of Funchal inhabited by the poorest Madeirans. Nowadays it's a prettified pedestrianized zone with cobblestones, antique gas lamps and brightly painted house fronts. After sundown, prospective diners are lured by the heady aromas of Portuguese fish stews and the plaintive strains of *fado* music emanating from the pavement cafés.

Beyond the **Capela do Corpo Santo** (on Rua de Santa Maria), founded by local fishermen at the end of the 15th century, is a larger church, the **Igreja do Socorro**. Take a peek inside at the splendid Baroque chancel arch – it chimes surprisingly well with the gaudily decorated altarpieces.

On the seaward side of these two monuments, the custard-yellow walls of the **Fortaleza de São Tiago** are the Zona Velha's most obvious landmark. The work of a Portuguese military engineer, Jerónimo Jorge, it was completed in 1637 and later enlarged. It looks disappointingly tame now that the marauding pirates have retreated for good, along with the garrison, leaving behind nothing more threatening than palms and potted plants. Inside there's a tiny **Museum of Contemporary Art** (Portuguese paintings from the 1960s onwards) and not much else, though there are great views of the harbour from the battlements. Just below is a stony beach, **Praia da Barreirinha**. You can swim here (the locals do) but you may prefer the sea-water lido just beyond the fort and accessible from the road by lift. The attendants will point you in the direction of the changing rooms and snack bars, where you can buy sandwiches, soft drinks and beer. The pool terraces are safe for children and there's a lifeguard on duty.

IBTAM

The initials stand for the Institute of Embroidery, Tapestry and Handicrafts, the body that regulates Madeira's traditional cottage industries. The museum at rua do Anadia 44 concentrates on embroidery and will appeal mainly to

THE JESUITS

The first Jesuit missionaries arrived on Madeira in 1569 following an invitation from King Sebastião of Portugal. Only a year later, French corsairs murdered their leader, Inácio de Azevedo. Undeterred, the shock troops of the Counter Reformation returned in 1572 with a charter to found a monastery and college (now the university). Substantial landowners, the order played a major role in wine cultivation, introducing new grape varieties such as Bual and Sercial on their estates around Fajã dos Padres.

One of Madeira's most colourful figures, Veitch was born in 1782 in Selkirk, although, according to one acquaintance, he shed all traces of his Scottish origins. Veitch made his fortune as a wine merchant supplying the Portuguese navy with Sercial. A sometime British consul, he was a constant embarrassment to the motherland on account of his womanizing and extravagant lifestyle. Churchgoers were scandalized by the shenanigans at his parties and by his endless succession of mistresses. In his spare time, Veitch was no mean architect, designing the **English Church**, the house on Rua 5 de Outobre (now the **Madeira Wine Institute**) and the **Quinta do Jardim da Serra** where he and his second wife are buried.

devotees interested in stitching and design. The displays date back to the late 19th century, when almost every able-bodied woman on the island was embroidering bedspreads, tablecloths and doilies to order. Open Monday–Friday 10:00–12:30 and 14:30–17:30, tel: 291 223 141.

Museu Henrique e Francisco Franco

Around the corner from IBTAM, on Rua João de Deus, look for an unusual building with a cylindrical bastion. It dates from the 1940s and was designed for the brothers, Henrique and Francisco Franco de Sousa, the former a painter, the latter, a sculptor. The Francos were born in Funchal and attended art school in Lisbon where they spent most of their working lives. Both benefited from the creative hothouse that was Paris in the 1920s and particularly from friendships with Picasso and Modigliani. The museum exhibits assorted landscapes and portraits by Henrique and sculptures by the more gifted Francisco whose commissions in Funchal include the monuments to Zarco and Henry the Navigator and the sculpture *The Sower* in the Parque de Santa Catarina. Open Tuesday–Saturday 10:00–12:30 and 14:00–17:30.

Quinta da Boa Vista

Just outside Funchal, on Rua da Boa Vista, are the Boa Vista ('Fine View') orchid nurseries, founded in the 1960s by a retired British fighter pilot and his wife, herself the daughter of a world authority on these beautiful flowers. The underlying philosophy of the Boa Vista enterprise is to preserve and propagate species otherwise threatened with extinction.

Thriving among the cymbidiums, cattleyas and slipper orchids (paphiopediums) are equally colourful displays of strelitzias, anthuriums, Latin American bromeliads and aloes. The nurseries are open Monday–Saturday 09:00–17:30 and are best seen from late November to the end of April.

HOTEL ZONE

This ribbon development of hotels and apartments to the west of Funchal starts near the Parque de Santa Catarina and continues for 5km (3 miles) in the direction of Câmara de Lobos. To walk into town from here can take anything from 30 minutes to an hour (don't be fooled by the brochures), but there's plenty of transport available – a regular bus service as well as taxis. The hotels advertise their cliff-top locations, sea views, lush green subtropical gardens and comprehensive sports

---

HOUSE OF LIGHT

One of Funchal's more unusual museums is dedicated to the history of electric power on Madeira. The location is the 'Casa de Luz' (literally 'House of Light'), an old power station in the centre of town, decommissioned in 1989 but given a new lease of life in 1997 when it was opened to the public. The exhibition spans more than a century, going back to the days of oil and kerosene, while the Science and Technology Hall uses interactive displays to make the subject accessible to the casual visitor. The museum is situated at rua Casa da Luz 2 and is open Tuesday–Sunday, 10:00–12:30 and 14:00–18:00, tel: 291 223 900.

Opposite: *The Fortaleza de São Tiago was an important link in the chain of the island's defences.*

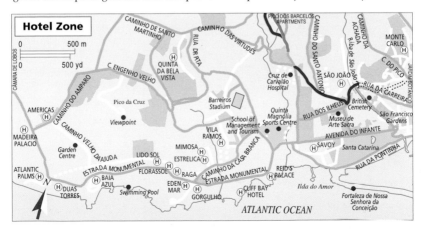

CYCLING

While Madeira's mountainous terrain hardly gives encouragement to amateur cyclists, Porto Santo is much easier to negotiate. To promote the sport on the island, the Madeira Sports Association organizes a round-the-island cycle race every July, about 50 riders taking part. Back on Madeira, Funchal town council has finally approved a scheme for a cycle lane on the Estrada Monumental, the highway which links the town centre with the hotel district and the beach at Praia Formosa.

Below: *The new motorway linking Funchal with Santa Catarina airport has cut journey times considerably.*

and leisure facilities. On the subject of views, it's only a short drive to one of Funchal's finest vantage points, **Pico dos Barcelos**. The most luxurious swimming pool is at the Savoy Hotel but the facilities at the public **lido** – an olympic pool with sea access, children's pool, etc., – will meet the needs of most families. There's a diving club based at the Atlantic Palms Hotel near the beach at **Praia Formosa** and tennis and squash courts (and swimming pool) in the lovely surroundings of the Quinta Magnólia municipal gardens.

Quinta Magnólia

A former country club, Quinta Magnólia is on Rua Dr Pita – follow the road north from Reid's Palace Hotel. Since 1980 it's been a public park, managed by the Madeiran regional government. You can make use of the plentiful sporting amenities (of which more later) or relax in the rambling subtropical gardens dreamt up by the original owner, the former American consul, and keen amateur botanist, T H Marsh. The villa is now home to the School of Hotel Management and Tourism – good news for visitors, as the students rustle up a four-course set lunch and afternoon tea at pleasingly affordable prices. (Book at least 24 hours ahead as tables are at a premium.) If you're the sporty type you'll be more interested in the tennis and squash courts, open-air heated swimming pool, putting green and jogging track. All the facilities are open to the public and there's a playground to keep the children amused. Open daily from 08:30–21:00 in summer; 08:30–17:00 in winter.

Reid's Palace Hotel

Reid's sits sedate and solitary on the rocky promontory it has occupied for more than a hundred years, as immovable as dowager settled into her favourite armchair and equally implacable in the face of change. Like Raffles in Singapore, Reid's has become an institution to the point where it's hard to imagine Madeira without it.

William Reid was the son of a near destitute Scottish crofter. He arrived in Funchal in 1836 with five pounds in his pocket and a burning ambition to succeed. From hiring out *quintas* to wealthy invalids, he moved on to hotels. Reid's was his dream and though he died a few years before the doors opened for the first time in 1891, his notion of what a luxury hotel should be lives on. While no longer *de rigeur*, guests tend to dress for dinner here, and afternoon tea is still served on the terrace with cucumber sandwiches, scones and clotted cream. And while every luxury hotel has its heated swimming pools (there are three), saunas (two) and gourmet restaurants (four), how many can boast a library or a billiards room? Were Sir Winston Churchill – a guest during the 1950s when he was recuperating from a stroke – to return today, one can imagine him feeling at home here. The same can probably be said for the other celebrities who have dropped in over the years: deposed emperors (Karl von Habsburg), former despots (General Batista of Cuba), poets (Maria Rainer Rilke), dramatists (George Bernard Shaw, who famously took dancing lessons, though well into his seventies), film stars (Gregory Peck and Roger Moore), missionaries (Albert Schweitzer), not forgetting British prime ministers (Lloyd George, Anthony Eden and Churchill). Madonna? – Reid's awaits!

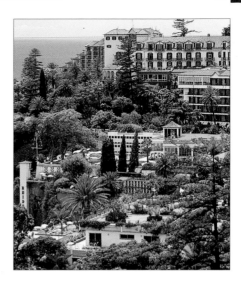

Above: *The stunning gardens below Reid's Hotel.*

BEST FLOWER BUYS

For-cut flowers, visit the stalls outside **Funchal Cathedral** or **Mercado dos Lavradores**. Orchids are the speciality of the **Quinta da Boa Vista** and the **Jardim Orquidéa** (Pregetters), and bulbs, plants and flowers are on sale in the Magnolia Flower Shop, in the gardens of the **Casino Park Hotel**. **A Estufa**, Madeira's largest commercial flower producer, packages flowers and plants for shipment by air. They have branches in Funchal (rua do Castanheiro 39 and Centro Comercial da Sé), the hotel zone (Eden Mar Hotel, Rua do Gorgulho) and Caniço.

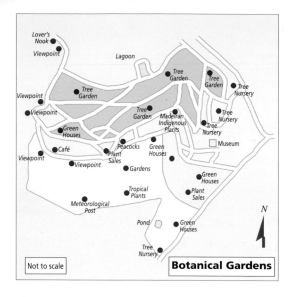

Not to scale

Botanical Gardens

Jardim Botânico ★★★

Take bus no. 29, 30 or 31 from the centre of Funchal to Caminho do Meio and the Botanical Gardens, one of Madeira's star attractions. The mansion in the former private estate, Quinta de Bom Successo, is now a small Natural History Museum. The gardens, spread over 5ha (12 acres) of terraced hillside, are dedicated to the cultivation and conservation of more than 2000 species of plants, trees and flowers from every continent. The exhibits are divided by region and genus and labelled in Latin and Portuguese (not English, unfortunately). There's something intoxicating about a place where everything thrives and proliferates, as here, where the warm air is heady with exotic fragrances. Among the flowers, you'll encounter azaleas, arum lilies, orchids and bromeliads, Japanese camellias, 'birds of paradise' (strelitzia), and Mexican 'tears of Christ'. It's hard to miss the palm garden and the towering giant known as *Phoenix canariensis*, while across the way, in the arboretum, are jacarandas, prickly dragon trees, ginkgos, sequoias and the majestic *Araucaria australiensis*, which can grow up to 60m (200ft) in its natural habitat.

One of the main purposes of the gardens is to breed and conserve plants indigenous to Madeira's coastline and laurel forest – geraniums and marguerites, wild orchids, and rare members of the subtropical *Cycadales* family, for example. These are gardens with something for everyone; depending on your taste, the highlight might be the cactus or rose garden, the herbarium with its stock of medicinal and aromatic plants, or the pergolas, cascades and escarpments. Agriculture is a special focus of study, which explains the abundance of tea plants, sweet potato and fruit trees. Whichever path you take there are numerous vantage points with sweeping views of Funchal and the coast. The gardens are open daily 09:00–18:00. Amenities include a café and shop.

Just below the gardens (separate entrance, same ticket) is the **Jardim dos Loiros**. From the squawks, screams and insane chattering you'll conclude (rightly) that this is a bird park – and a 'must see' if you have children. The preening stars are the parrots, lories and conures, but they're all rumbustious extroverts, from the Australian parakeets and the absurd Ghanaian hornbills to the mynah birds, cockatoos, lovebirds and macaws. Bring earplugs!

Take the side turning below the bird park (Rua Pita da Silva) and after 100m (109yd) you'll come to the **Jardim Orquídea**, the orchid nurseries of the Pregetter family. Strictly speaking the plants here bloom year-round, but for the best displays come between November and early April. There are more than 400 varieties of orchid, including rare native species like *Dachtylorhiza foliosa* and equally colourful imports from Brazil, India and New Guinea. You can watch them being cultivated in the laboratory before shopping for a plant to take home as a memento of your visit. Open daily 09:00–18:00.

SOCCER STAR

Harry Hinton was 18 when, in 1875, he made history by organizing the first soccer game in Portugal. It took place in Camacha, next to the Café O Relógio (a wall plaque now commemorates the event). Hinton remained closely associated with the game for the rest of his life. He was present in 1910 at the historic opening match between the newly formed Madeiran club, Marítimo, and an English scratch team (the Portuguese creating a minor sensation by winning 2–1). Hinton provided a cup in his name in the 1920s and was made honorary president of Marítimo in 1942. Today the club, which plays at the Estádio dos Barreiros in Funchal, is one of the strongest sides in the Portuguese first division.

Below: *Topiary Garden, one of the delights in the Jardim Botânico.*

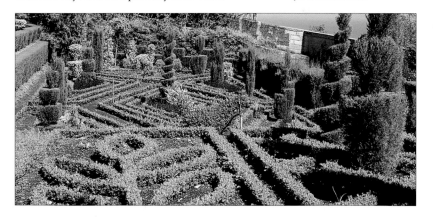

Funchal at a Glance

Weather-wise, Funchal is pleasant at any time of year. July, August and September are the sunniest months, though September can be wet. It's warm in June but there's more cloud. August is the busiest month as many mainland visitors arrive for the summer vacation. The Christmas season (8 December to 6 January) is especially lively, with street and harbour illuminations, concerts, crib displays and one of Europe's most spectacular firework displays to mark New Year.

Road links between Santa Catarina airport and Funchal are good. A taxi will take about 25 minutes to cover the 22km (14 miles). There is a bus service, but it's not very reliable (journey time is around 45 minutes).

Funchal is easily negotiated on foot but be prepared for some uphill walking. There are two **bus** stations (east-bound and westbound) for accessing other parts of the island. (Timetables and destination information are available from tourist offices.) Town buses are orange. Tourist passes (valid for your stay) are a good idea if you intend making frequent use of buses. They are on sale from kiosks on Avenida do

Mar, where you will also find bus stops. **Taxis** are metered but there are fixed rates for out-of-town journeys – check with the driver about prices.

LUXURY
Reid's Palace, Estrada Monumental, tel: 291 717 030, fax: 291 717 033. The last word in Colonial-style luxury, Reid's is an institution, the emphasis being on tradition and formality. Reid's offers surprisingly generous out-of-season packages.
Savoy, Avenida do Infante, tel: 291 222 031, fax: 291 223 103. A famous name with a reputation to match, the Savoy's facilities rival those of Reid's, the swimming pool having the edge.
Casino Park Hotel, Rua Imperatriz D. Amélia, tel: 291 33 111, fax: 291 232 076. Visually a bit of an eyesore, this large hotel near the Santa Catarina Park has a good location with views overlooking the bay.
Cliff Bay Resort Hotel, Estrada Monumental, tel: 291 707 700, fax: 291 762 525. Typical 5-star hotel; facilities include outdoor and indoor pools, health club, tennis courts and sauna.
Hotel Monte Carlo, Calçada da Saúde, tel: 291 226 131, fax: 291 226 134. A little way out of town, this grand old building has its own pool and matchless sea views.

MID-RANGE
Eden Mar, Rua do Gorgulho, tel: 291 709 700, fax: 291 761 966. In the medium price range but with excellent amenities including a huge pool, a sauna and a jacuzzi.
Windsor, Rua das Hortas, tel: 291 233 083, fax: 291 233 080. Friendly hotel in excellent downtown location, with small rooftop swimming pool.
Quinta da Bela Vista, Caminho Avista Navios 4, tel: 291 706 400. About 15 minutes from the centre by car, this attractive mansion has a delightful garden setting.

BUDGET
Pension Astoria, Rua João Gago, tel: 291 223 820, fax: 291 227 229. The location near the cathedral can hardly be bettered; clean and well run.

LUXURY
A Morgadinha, rua da Levada de São João 4, tel: 291 740 920. This hotel-restaurant is not easy to find, but worth the trouble for the wonderful Goan and international dishes.
Casa Velha do Palheiro, rua Imperatriz D. Amélia 69, tel: 291 205 600. Expensive, but superb food and the menu is more imaginative than most.
Les Faunes, Reid's Hotel, tel: 291 717 030. *Haute cuisine* at prices to match, smart dress is essential.

Funchal at a Glance

MID-RANGE

Arsénio's, rua de Santa Maria 169, tel: 291 224 007. This seafood restaurant, best known for its *fado* music, caters largely for tourists.

Dom Filet, rua do Favila 7, tel: 291 764 426, fax: 291 763 826. Upmarket steak-house specializing in *espetada*.

Mar Azul, Marina, tel: 291 230 079. Probably the best bet on the seafront if you're looking for reasonably priced meat and seafood dishes with a touch of local colour.

O Jango, rua de Santa Maria 166, tel: 291 221 840. Cosy family-run restaurant, popular with locals and visitors alike; fresh fish a speciality.

O Tapassol, rua Dom Carlos I, 62, tel: 291 225 023. Old town restaurant with rooftop terrace, specializing in Madeiran dishes.

BUDGET

Hong Kong, Olimpo shopping centre, Avenida do Infante, tel: 291 228 181. Not the most attractive of settings, but surprisingly good Chinese cuisine.

SHOPPING

Casa do Turista (Avenida do Mar) is the main outlet for souvenirs, otherwise try Rua João Tavira and other streets around the cathedral. There are two main shopping centres: Eden Mar (Rua do Gorgulho) in the hotel zone, and Infante (Avenida Arriaga) near the marina.

TOURS AND EXCURSIONS

Eurofun, Centro Comercial Olimpo, Avenida do Infante, Funchal, tel: 291 228 638, fax: 291 228 620. Boat trips, jeep safaris, mountain biking, rock climbing, etc.

MAPA, (Montanhismo Animação e Práticas de Aventura), Urbanização das Neves, Funchal, tel: 291 203 360, fax: 291 203 368. Walks, trekking, jeep safaris, mountain biking, rock climbing, etc.

Turivema, (Turismo Verde e Ecológico da Madeira), Edifício Baía, Loja 1 R/C Bloco Leste, Estrada Monumental 187, tel: 291 766 109, fax: 291 766 210.

Most **bus companies** arrange excursions to tourist attractions (*see* bus stations for details). For outdoor activities, including canyoning and hang-gliding, contact **Terras de Aventura & Turismo**, Caminho do Amparo 25, tel: 291 766 818, fax: 291 761 018.

Heliatlantis offers bird's-eye tours of Funchal and the island by helicopter. Tel: 291 232 882, fax: 291 232 804, or go to Estrada do Pontinha (Cais dos Contentores), between the marina and the harbour.

USEFUL CONTACTS

Tourist Information: Avenida Arriaga 18, tel: 291 211 900, fax: 291 232 151. Open 09:00–20:00. Website: www.madeiratourism.org CC Monumental Lido, Estrada Monumental 284, tel: 291 775 254. Open Monday–Friday 10:00–13:00 and 14:30–18:00, Saturday 10:00–12:30. Funchal Harbour, tel: 291 236 161.

Car rental: Avis, Santa Catarina airport, tel: 291 524 392. Hertz, Santa Catarina airport, tel: 291 523 040. O Moinho, Estrada Monumental, tel: 291 762 123.

Taxis: Largo do Municipio 291 222 000. Avenida do Mar 291 224 588.

Diving: Scorpio Divers, Complexo Balnear do Lido 9000, Funchal, tel: (mobile) 966 861 846. Centro de Mergulho Golfinho Hotel, Cliff Bay, Estrada Monumental, tel: 291 707 700, fax: 291 762 525, website: www.cliffbay.com

Tennis: Rua Dr Pita, Anexo Barreiros, tel: 291 763 237, fax: 291 763 930.

Horse Riding: Associação Hipica da Madeira, Quinta Vila Alpires, Caminho dos Pretos, tel: 291 792 582.

Sea Fishing: Costa do Sol Marina do Funchal, tel: 291 224 390, fax: 291 235 735. Nautisantos Sport Fishing Madeira Marina do Funchal, tel/fax: 291 231 312, website: www.nautisantosfishing.com

Dolphin and whale watching excursions: Katherine B Captain Peter Bristow Quinta das Malvas, rua da Levada de Santa Luzia 124, Funchal, tel: 291 220 334, fax: 291 229 896.

3
Western Madeira

Western Madeira is possibly the least known part of the island. One reason is that until fairly recently it was remote and inaccessible – for example, until the 1960s, the beautiful coastal hamlet of **Paúl do Mar** (now the island's surfing 'capital') could only be reached by boat. Everything changed a few years ago with the opening of the expressway between **Funchal** and **Ribeira Brava**, cutting the journey time from one hour to just 15 minutes. Coach tours and boat excursions visit this busy little resort. Beyond Ribeira Brava the coast road threads through remarkably fertile countryside, over hillsides planted with bananas and vines. Along the way you can experience the famous sunsets at **Ponta do Sol**, visit the lighthouse at **Ponta do Pargo** (the island's most westerly point), or stop for lunch at one of several picturesque fishing villages – **Jardim do Mar** for example. Another strong suit of the region is its churches and chapels, many of them off the beaten track but worth exploring for their architecture, artistic treasures and splendid *Mudéjar* ceilings.

The main road north from Ribeira Brava follows the course of Madeira's most impressive river valley, climbing to the *miradouro* (lookout) at **Encumeada** and the fringes of the **Paúl da Serra** plateau before making the spectacular descent to **São Vicente**. The coastal scenery here, towards the resort village of **Porto Moniz**, is breathtaking. Awesome Atlantic breakers pound the basalt beaches, flooding the coves and rocky inlets and submerging the treacherous reefs, a perennial hazard to shipping in the area.

ATLANTIC OCEAN

Madeira

São Vicente

Ribeira Brava

FUNCHAL

Don't Miss

*** **Boca da Encumeada:** *miradouro* with views of the north coast and Serra de Agua.
*** **Rabaçal:** enchanting scenery as well as good *levada* walking.
** **Grutas de São Vicente:** volcanic caves formed more than 400,000 years ago.
* **Ponta do Pargo:** the most westerly point; wild and desolate.
* **Porto Moniz:** coastal resort with swimming pool and fish restaurants.

Opposite: *Ponta do Pargo, the most westerly point of the island.*

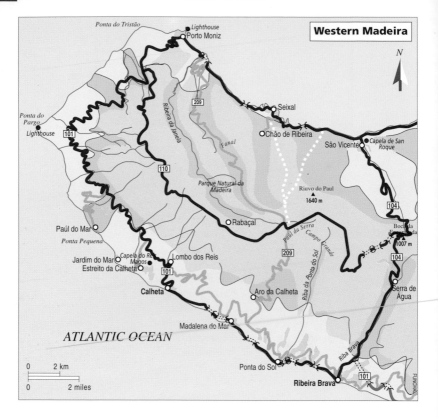

Opposite: *The lighthouse at Ponta do Pargo.*

PONTA DO PARGO ★

Ponta do Pargo means 'Dolphin Point', a reference to the dolphin-fish (*pargos*) still caught in local waters. There's not much to see in this remote village but if you're looking for peace and quiet, you've come to the right place – contact the tourist offices in Funchal or Porto Moniz for information about bungalows and holiday lets in the vicinity. Once a year, on or around the third weekend in September, the village puts on its glad rags for the Apple Festival (it's said that sailors can detect the aroma far out at sea). Ponta do Pargo is the most westerly point of the island – next stop, America. As you leave the village, look for the turning to the **lighthouse** (*farol*) and follow the signs for about 3km (2 miles) along the track. The outlook to sea from the clifs is well worth the detour.

There's a popular coastal walk following the *levada* from **Ponta do Pargo** to **Calheta**, with uninterrupted views of the Atlantic Ocean on one side and the ridges of the **Paúl da Serra** on the other. You'll need to bring sunglasses and sunblock as the path is south-facing with only occasional shade from pine and eucalyptus.

PONTA DO SOL

In days gone by, African slaves worked the sugar plantations around Ponta do Sol, inspiring the 'carriers' dance, patterned on the movements of labourers jogging to and from the mills, laden with heavy baskets. The most prominent slave owner was the Flemish sugar merchant and friend of Columbus, Jeannin Esmerandt (João Esmeraldo) who built a country estate for himself here; it still survives, though in a much-altered form. The parish church is dedicated to Our Lady of Light (Nossa Senhora da Luz) – a pointer, perhaps, to the town's reputation for basking in year-round sunlight. The wooden *Mudéjar* ceiling dates from the time of King Manuel I, as does the green ceramic font and the exquisite *azulejos* (hand-decorated tiles). Follow the cobbled streets down to the beach where you can pick your way across the pebbles for a cooling dip; alternatively, take a stroll along the promenade.

DIVING WRECK

Several diving schools visit the wreck of the *Bowbelle*, 25m (82ft) beneath the waves off **Ponta do Sol**. The boat has a tragic history. On 20 August 1989 the *Bowbelle*, a gravel dredger on London's River Thames, was involved in a collision with a pleasure cruiser, the *Marchioness*, resulting in the death of 51 of the 131 people on board, mostly young people attending a party. Several years later, the *Bowbelle* was sold to a Madeiran company where it was registered under a new name, the *Bom Rei*. In March 1996 the *Bom Rei* broke in two and sank during a storm, one crew member losing his life in the incident.

ROOTS

Though the celebrated American author, John Dos Passos (1896–1970), was born in Chicago, his grandparents came from **Ponta do Sol**. Dos Passos deals almost exclusively with urban and industrial themes in novels like *Manhattan Transfer* (1925) and the *USA* trilogy (1930–38). Perhaps it was a lingering affinity for his ancestral home that induced him to pay Ponta do Sol a brief visit when he was already in his sixties – a plaque on the wall of the town hall recalls the occasion. Having paid his respects, he returned to his suite in **Reid's Hotel**.

HENRIQUE ALEMÃO

'Henry the German' was, in fact, King Wladislaw III of Poland, who gave up his throne after suffering a crushing defeat at the Battle of Varna in 1414. His plans to make a round-the-world pilgrimage were scuppered when he was shipwrecked off the coast of Madeira, but his fortunes improved after **Zarco** made him a gift of land near **Madalena do Mar**. It turned out that Wladislaw was a born farmer, and the local community prospered as a result. Wladislaw married the daughter of a Portuguese nobleman but died tragically when a landslide off **Cabo Girão** destroyed his ship as he was about to set out on a journey to Portugal. We know what he looked like because he appears in the painting, *Santa Ana and São Joaquim*, in the **Museu de Arte Sacra**.

THE WEST COAST

The stretch of coastline between **Ponta do Sol** and **Ponta do Pargo** makes a rewarding drive which you could complete in a morning or afternoon, even with detours.

Bananas are the mainstay of the economy, planted on the stepped hillside terraces known as *poios*. These are not the *bananas da terrá* (plantain) introduced to the island in the 16th century, but the small and succulent Chinese dwarf variety produced for export.

The parish of **Madalena do Mar** was founded in 1457 by the enigmatic Henrique Alemão (*see* panel), who is buried in the church. The village is little more than a ribbon of houses strung along the seafront. There's usually plenty of room on the long strip of pebbly sand, where you'll find cafés, shower facilities and, likely as not, volleyball enthusiasts. Just past the village there's a side turning which winds tortuously in the direction of **Arco da Calheta**, from where there are good coastal views.

There are three interesting churches in the area. **Nossa Senhora de Loreto** (Our Lady of Loreto) dates from the 18th century, but some of the original Manueline features can still be seen – the south portal, the font and the *Mudéjar* roof, since over-painted. In

Calheta parish church the distinctive geometrical patterning on the ceiling (*alfarge* in Portuguese) has survived intact – only Funchal Cathedral has a finer example. Before you leave, take a closer look at the beautiful silver and ebony tabernacle in the sanctuary.

A little way past the village, the coast road turns inland towards **Estreito da Calheta**. Keep an eye out here for signs to **Lombo dos Reis** and the **Chapel of the Three Kings** (Capela dos Reis Magos) where the coat of arms of the founder, Francisco de Gouveia, is emblazoned above the entrance. If the

chapel isn't open, ask for the key next door – *o chave, se faz favor* – so you can see the sumptuous oak altarpiece depicting the journey of the Magi. This work was commissioned early in the 16th century from artists in Antwerp, more evidence of the cross-cultural fertilization born of the sugar trade.

On leaving Estreito da Calheta, take the turning to **Jardim do Mar** (literally 'garden of the sea'). This picture-postcard pretty fishing village hosted the World Surfing Championships in January 2001, drawing competitors from as far afield as Brazil and Australia. Here and in the neighbouring villages of **Paúl do Mar** and **Ponta Pequena**, Atlantic rollers of awesome dimensions – 5m (16ft) plus – break over the black basalt shingle. Ride these waves if you dare!

Water sports enthusiasts should also check out the **Calheta Beach Hotel**, about 10 minutes from the village.

Above: *The painted ceiling in the parish church of Arco da Calheta.*
Opposite: *Volleyball players making the most of the evening sunshine on Calheta beach.*

Right: *A statue of Zarco, erected to commemorate the 500th anniversary of the discovery of Madeira.*
Opposite: *The splendid Church of São Bento in Ribeira Brava boasts a number of original Manueline features.*

MANUELINE ARCHITECTURE

During the reign of Manuel I (1495–1521) Portugal gave birth to its own, distinctive architectural style, inspired by the voyages of discovery and funded by the vast wealth pouring into the country from the New World. The most distinctive aspect of the Manueline style is the embellishment of doorways, arches, window frames and capitals, often with nautical motifs. Examples on Madeira include Funchal Cathedral, the Church of the Incarnation, Funchal, the Church of São Bento in Ribeira Brava (font and pulpit), the parish church at Santa Cruz (portals), and Quinta das Cruzes (window frames preserved in the garden).

RIBEIRA BRAVA

Thanks to the new expressway this small, touristy resort fringed with banana plantations is a mere 15 minutes away by car from Funchal. If you have the time though, it's worth considering the boat excursion which makes a stop here via **Câmara de Lobos** and the spectacular cliffs at **Cabo Girão**.

The name 'Ribeira Brava' means 'wild river'. If you're here in July and August when the river bed is covered with vegetation, even the notion of a torrent is inconceivable. Yet it's a fact that, over time measured in millennia, the huge ravine running parallel with the road to **São Vicente** is the work of this fitfully mighty waterway.

The one tourist sight is the **Church of São Bento** (St Benedict). The Baroque bell tower with its overlarge clock, checkerboard steeple and decorative balusters has a slightly surreal aspect, though it was founded in the 15th century. Things to look out for in the cool, pristine interior include the original Manueline arches, the carvings on the 16th-century font (near the entrance), and the pulpit, ornamented with sailors' knot motifs.

Ribeira Brava is a good place to shop for gifts: not just the predictable mugs and T-shirts but wooden toboggans and caravels, glassware, wickerwork, embroidered place mats, tablecloths, etc. The harbour on the other hand is a disappointment, as is the rather charmless concrete promenade – the two are connected by a tunnel in the rock.

Ribeira Brava's red-letter day is the feast of St Peter (29 June), when garlands of paper flowers are strung across the cobbled streets and revellers from across the island arrive by boat to cook barbecues of skewered beef (*espetada*) on the stony beach.

PORTO MONIZ *

A small seaside resort 75km (47 miles) northwest of Funchal, Porto Moniz is one of the remotest points on the island but it's also one of the busiest, at least at lunchtimes when coach parties descend on the hotel complex behind the promenade. The seafood restaurants are the main draw here – you'll need to book ahead or

---

ETHNOGRAPHICAL MUSEUM

The **Museu Etnográfico da Madeira** in Ribeira Brava offers a fascinating insight into the history of the island's trades and handicrafts including weaving, farming, viticulture and fishing. Local craftsmen give demonstrations. The 16th-century building was formerly a rum distillery and sugar cane mill and you can still see some of the original equipment, notably the water wheel. There is a café on the premises and a shop selling souvenirs. Rua de São Francisco 24, tel: 291 952 598. Open Tuesday–Sunday 10:00–12:30, 14:00–18:00; closed on holidays.

PONTA DO TRISTÃO

Porto Moniz was originally
known as Ponta do Tristão
but was renamed for
Francisco Moniz, a nobleman
from the Algarve and a
relative of Zarco's through
marriage. Moniz built a
chapel on the coast, dedicat-
ing it to Nossa Senhora da
Conceição. Some time after
his death, in 1535, it was
moved to a more sheltered
site after Moroccan corsairs
began using the village as a
jumping-off point for raids
on **Porto Santo**. The
present church was
completed in 1668.

come early to be sure of a table. It's a short, but bracing
stroll from the bus stop (last service to São Vicente,
14:30) along the seafront, via the tourist office and the
excellent gift shop, Bordarte Souvenirs, where you can
buy everything from ornamental banana trees to
anthologies of Madeiran folk music. These 'Songs of the
Sea', with their tales of hazard and shipwreck, were
inspired by the treacherous coastline – the volcanic
rocks, like the armour-plated backs of stegosauruses,
seem to lurk in the spume. The salt spray permeates the
air and is a potential danger to the crops growing on the
hillsides. The best defence, local farmers have found, is
to build screens of heather, bracken, brushwood or what-
ever else comes to hand.

If you feel the need for a swim, Porto Moniz boasts
one of the most attractive lidos on the island. The
natural lava pools are connected by a series of concrete
bridges and walkways, making access easy for young
and old alike.

SEIXAL

If you've come to Madeira to relax, this sleepy, unself-
conscious hamlet – call it a village at a push – is just the
place. It's also an ideal base for exploring the rugged
north coast and the enchanting hinterland around Fanal.
Seixal makes its living not from fishing, as you might
first suspect, but from agriculture. The local grape,
Sercial, produces the driest of Madeiran wines, and is

Below: *The view from
one of the numerous*
miradouros *on the
winding road leading
down to Porto Moniz.*

grown on the precipitous slopes to the rear of the village. If you've a head for heights, take a closer look at the vines, trained over raised trestles to protect them from the fungal diseases that thrive on damp soil. Subtropical fruits, including mangoes, avocados, figs and sugar apples, all flourish in the fertile Seixal valley.

The village offers little to tourists but itself. As the twisting lanes and passageways drop towards the sea, most of them turn out to be cul-de-sacs, an invitation to linger and enjoy the charm of the houses, decorated with *azulejo* shrines to the Virgin or St Vincent, and brightly painted chimneys that resemble miniature campaniles.

From the quay an unusual rock formation reaches into the sea like an outstretched hand. Steps lead down to the water but the fishermen won't thank you for spoiling their sport; in any case, swimming is not recommended – huge ray fish have been spotted only a few metres from the shore and currents are strong and unpredictable. The rock pool *piscina* nearby is fed directly by the sea, which swells and foams ominously near the stepladders at high tide. The pick of Seixal's restaurants is **O Aquario** where, as the name suggests, octopus and other seafood feature prominently on the menu.

Above: *Porto Moniz's natural rock pools have been transformed into a splendid lido.*

SUGAR MILL

Sugar production in the Calheta region began back in the 15th century, though there are few signs of it today. However, the **Engenho da Calheta** is an early 20th-century mill which distills sugar into rum. You can sample the product after exploring the distillery at your leisure. The mill is located next to the Igreja Matriz (Parish Church), tel: 291 822 264. Open Monday–Friday, 08:00–19:00.

Blue and pink acanthus brighten the road to **Châo de Ribeira**, an EU-funded agricultural development about 3km (2 miles) above the village. Women in headscarves, carrying cabbages and potatoes from the market gardens, will greet you along the way. The restaurant at Châo has unpredictable opening times so if you're planning on lunch, pack a picnic – there are tables waiting for you.

FANAL

One of Madeira's unsung beauty spots, Fanal could be an enjoyable half-day excursion from Porto Moniz or Seixal. Since 1982 this thickly wooded mountain ridge, more than 1000m (3280ft) above sea level, has been administered by the National Park of Madeira which conserves the endemic flora and fauna, including endangered species like the *Freira da Madeira* (laurel pigeon). To get to Fanal take the EN209 from Porto Moniz, but check your suspension beforehand as this 'road' is little more than a track in places. Leave the car near the Forestry Station and relish the stark grandeur of a landscape untamed and unaltered in a thousand years. If you'd rather not make the trip on your own (mists descend regularly), Madeira Trails of Adventure organize jeep safaris to Fanal, stopping en route to see the volcanic crater.

THE NORTH COAST ROAD

The 19km (12-mile) stretch of road from São Vicente to Porto Moniz makes an exhilarating, if demanding, drive (allow between 45 minutes and one hour). Period photographs document the formidable obstacles that had to be overcome in the building of this highway. It took men with an enviable head for heights and the agility of mountain goats more than 16 years to carve the cliff tunnels from the bare rock.

Before you set out, bear in mind the rules of the road here – give way to oncoming traffic at all times and remember to drive slowly, as there's an unnerving number of hairpin bends ahead. Sea spray from the pounding Atlantic breakers and the cascades from the cliff face, which land indiscriminately on any vehicle in their path, are some of the hazards you'll have to face. Be as phlegmatic about the latter as the locals, who think of it as a free car wash!

> ### QUINTAS
>
> Most of the surviving *quintas* (out-of-town estates) date from the late 17th century onwards and were built by prominent local families, or foreign (mainly British) settlers. Many were highly productive agricultural estates with vineyards, orchards and vegetable gardens. During the 19th and early 20th centuries many *quintas* were rented out as holiday homes to foreign royals and other members of the glitterati. While **Quinta das Cruzes** is the only villa open to the public, many of the gardens may be visited: **Quinta Magnólia**, **Quinta do Palheiro Ferreiro**, **Quinta Monte Palace** and **Quinta Vigia** (now part of the **Santa Catarina Gardens**).

Opposite: *A rugged shoreline, typical of Madeira's north coast.*
Left: *Cliff tunnels like this one, on the North Coast Road, were hewn from the rock by hand.*

SÃO VICENTE

This attractive village lies at the foot of a spectacular, steep-sided valley. If you're approaching from the coast road you'll notice a tiny chapel emerging from a single block of basalt at the mouth of the river. The **Capela de San Roque** was built in 1694 and marks the spot where St Vincent is said to have made a miraculous appearance. Bleak and windswept, the beach is stony and ill-suited to swimming, though the hotel restaurants at the far end are worth investigating if you're on the lookout for an evening meal. The core of the village is a little way inland (just follow the course of the river). Palm trees peer down on a 17th-century parish church dedicated to St Vincent. The interior is the usual Baroque confection, gaudily painted and with lashings of scrolled gold leaf for decorative effect. There's little to shatter the peace and quiet here – the bandstand on the forecourt is usually empty. Occasionally, however, people do emerge from behind the dazzling, green-shuttered houses to do the shopping or tend the tubs of flowers and potted plants that add a dash of colour to the cobbled lanes.

There's a supermarket if you need to stock up on essentials, as well as a selection of cafés and small restaurants. It's a 15-minute walk from the village to the

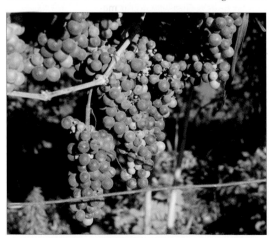

Right: *Grapes from São Vicente, now the second largest wine-producing area on the island.*

Grutas de São Vicente. This cave system was formed some 400,000 years ago when the volcanoes of the Paúl da Serra erupted, spewing streams of molten lava down the mountainside, hollowing out the melting rock in the process. The galleries were discovered by an English visitor in 1855. They extend for more than 700m (2296ft), although only about 70m (230ft) is open to the public (allow about half an hour for a guided tour).

Inside, the temperature is constant. Plant seeds carried in by water seeping through the rock grow only because of the presence of artificial light. These caves too have stalactites, only here they never grow – they were formed in an instant when the drops of molten rock froze on the spot.

Above: *Getting about Madeira can be a time-consuming business as there are many natural barriers to negotiate.*

PAÚL DA SERRA

Bleak, inhospitable yet strangely beautiful, Paúl da Serra is a windswept moorland plateau 1200–1500m (3937–4920ft) above sea level. Sheep, goats and cattle graze among the clumps of ferns and heather but there are few signs of human habitation. It's usually freezing cold up here – if you intend getting out of the car, take a jumper. Before you set out, check on the weather – you'll see little or nothing when the mist descends and the shepherds take shelter in mountain caves. If you have the right equipment (hiking boots, warm clothing, an anorak, and water) and want to make the trip from Funchal, take a taxi to the statue of Cristo Rei (Christ the King) on the edge of the Campo Grande then follow the *levada* channel. It's an exhilarating feeling skirting the plateau, volcanic peaks in one direction and a panoramic sweep of the coastal fishing villages of Madalena do Mar, Calheta, Ponta do Sol, etc., in the other.

RABAÇAL ***

Flanked by the peaks of the Paúl da Serra, the luxuriant scenery of the Rabaçal valley has always enchanted visitors. The location is a special favourite with hikers, as not one but three *levadas* converge to feed the hydro-electric power station at Calheta. Rabaçal is only accessible by car so if you don't want to bring your own vehicle, hire a taxi for the day – it's worth it. The starting point for walks is the government forestry station where the amenities include toilets, barbecue stands and picnic tables. It's possible to leave and rejoin the system at several points along the way, depending on how far you want to walk. For a gentle stroll, follow the **Levada do Risco** from the car park for 15 minutes and you'll arrive at the falls, a spectacular cataract which plunges 100m (330ft) over a sheer cliff into the ravine below. The local humidity accounts for the ragged curtain of lichen clinging to the rock. The **Levada dos 25 Fontes** leads to another beauty spot – a small clearing in the primeval laurel forest where ribbons of water seep from hidden clefts in the rock, before tumbling into an emerald pool. (Allow about an hour for the round trip.) If you have extra reserves of energy, double back and take the turn-off to the **Levada do Rocha Vermelha** which traverses the lower reaches of the Rabaçal gorge en route to the valley of the Ribeira de Janela. Here you'll encounter beauty of a different kind as you leave the laurel forest behind for a more open landscape of grassy hillsides and heath trees.

BOCA DA ENCUMEADA ***

Midway along the north-south highway connecting **Ribeira Brava** with **São Vicente** is the **Encumeada Pass**,

> **TAKE A PICNIC**
>
> There are few more enjoyable places for picnicking than Madeira with its spectacular scenery. Some choice spots are the Bica da Cana observation point in the Paúl da Serra, the government rest house near the car park at Rabaçal (also in the Paúl da Serra), the woods at Ribeiro Frio, and the Queimadas rest house at the beginning of the *levada* walk to Caldeirão Verde.

Opposite: *The hillside village of São Vicente is sheltered from coastal winds.*

Below: *Typically rugged terrain in the Paúl da Serra – desolate, all but uninhabited and frequently shrouded in mist.*

WALKERS' 'BIBLE'

Pat and John Underwood's trailblazing book, *Landscapes of Madeira*, first appeared in 1980 and is still an invaluable guide to *levada* walking on the island, with incredibly detailed maps, route marches and practical advice. You'll find it on sale in bookshops in Funchal; alternatively visit the website: www.sunflowerbooks.co.uk

one of the best-known *miradouros* (lookouts) on the island. The vantage point is 1004m (3294ft) high but what you see from here depends very much on the weather – whorls of cloud may obscure the view below even as you enjoy bright sunlight on the ledge. On the other hand, strike it lucky and much of the northern coastline unfolds in one direction, and the Serra de Agua in the other. There's a small café with picnic tables near the car park, but if you've brought lunch with you there are choicer spots in the woods. Keep the camera handy because there are more *miradouros* as the road descends south to the **Pousada dos Vinháticos Hotel** – make a reservation to be sure of a table in the aptly named Panorama restaurant. Cosily ensconced in the valley below is the village of **Serra de Agua**, literally 'sawmill', where there are several small hotels and bungalows, should you wish to stay overnight. If you're feeling energetic, there's a great walk from Encumeada to **Boca da Corrida** with rewarding views of **Curral das Freitas** and several mountain peaks, including **Pico Grande** and **Pico de Serradinho**. Only moderately difficult, it will take you about 3½ hours to complete – Turivema organize a walk along this route.

Below: *The river valley of Serra de Agua is a majestic sight.*

Western Madeira at a Glance

July–September are best for festivals: 'Week by the Sea', Porto Moniz, the first week of August.

Grape harvest, villages along the north and west coast, first two weeks of September.

Apple festival, Ponta do Pargo, usually the third weekend in September.

Council week (gastronomy), Câmara de Lobos, first week of July.

GETTING THERE

Buses leave from the Rodoeste bus station on Rua Ribeira João Gomes, Funchal, for Ribeira Brava, São Vicente, Seixal, Porto Moniz, Boca de Encumeada, Ponta do Pargo, Ponta do Sol and Calheta. The **expressway** from Funchal is the quickest way of reaching Ribeira Brava by car (15 minutes); **boat excursions** from Funchal marina also stop here.

GETTING AROUND

The easiest is to hire a car or taxi. Bus services, while reliable, are infrequent. In Porto Moniz the private cabs in the main square tend to overcharge.

WHERE TO STAY

MID-RANGE

Estalegem Onda Azul, Calheta, tel: 291 820 300, fax: 291 820 301. The name 'Blue Wave' is appropriate as this small hotel with restaurant is just a stone's throw from the beach.

Hotel Jardim do Mar, Sítio da Piedade Jardim do Mar, tel: 291 823 616, fax: 291 823 617. A pleasant hotel located in one of the loveliest villages on the island.

Pensão Brisa Mar, Sítio do Cais, Seixal, tel: 291 854 476, fax: 291 854 477. Friendly family-run hotel with excellent sea views.

Pensão Praia Mar, Sítio do Calhau São Vicente, tel: 291 842 383. Small, but attractive seafront hotel with comfortable rooms.

Sol Mar, Perto da Ponte, Seixal, tel: 291 854 854, fax: 291 854 855. Small cliff-top hotel with restaurant, serving typical Madeiran dishes.

BUDGET

Residencial Calhau, Porto Moniz, tel: 291 853 104, fax: 291 853 443. Comfortable rooms, just a short walk from the swimming pool, with restaurants on hand.

WHERE TO EAT

MID-RANGE

Orca, Porto Moniz, tel: 291 850 000 or 291 850 000. Possibly the best of several seafood restaurants in the square behind the pool. Very busy at lunch times.

O Virgilio, São Vicente, tel: 291 842 467. Seafront restaurant patronized by locals – always a good recommendation.

Panorama restaurant, Pousada dos Vinháticos, Serra

de Agua, tel: 291 952 148. Hotel restaurant specializing in homely cooking including nourishing soups, and meat dishes such as *espetada*.

BUDGET

O Aquario, Seixal, tel: 291 854 396. One of the best seafood restaurants in the area.

TOURS AND EXCURSIONS

MAPA, *see* page 59.

Turivema, *see* page 59.

NATURA, Actividades Turisticas, PO Box 4072, Funchal Codex, tel: 291 236 015, fax: 238 652, website: www.natura-travel.com Organizes walking tours.

Heliatlantis, *see* page 59.

Aerogene, Sítio das Achadas de Santo Antão 9370-011 Arco da Calheta, tel: 291 827 634, website: www.madeira. airbase.de. Hang-gliding and para-gliding.

Diving: Clube Naval do Seixal Cais do Seixal, Porto Moniz, tel: 965 013 572.

USEFUL CONTACTS

Tourist Offices: Ribeira Brava, Forte de São Bento, tel: 291 951 675. Open Monday–Friday 09:00–12:30, 14:00–17:00, Saturday 09:30–12:00. Porto Moniz, promenade, tel: 291 852 594. Open Monday–Friday 10:00–15:00, Saturday 12:00–15:00.

Taxis: Ribeira Brava, tel: 291 952 349, Calheta, tel: 291 822 129, Ponta do Sol, tel: 291 972 110.

4
Central Madeira

It is said that when Queen Isabella of Spain asked Columbus to describe one of her new island possessions, he replied by taking a piece of paper and crumpling it in his hands. The story probably relates to Jamaica but could equally well apply to the landscape of central Madeira, its chain of volcanic peaks forming a stupendous natural barrier between the northern and southern parts of the island. Reaching them is relatively straightforward, though the road from Funchal is among the most tortuous on the island. Beyond the genteel suburb of **Monte**, with its famous twin-towered church and Tropical Garden, lies the Poiso pass and the turn-off to Madeira's third highest mountain, **Pico do Arieiro**. The views from the summit (accessible by car) are a highlight of any visit. There are more views to the west, from the *miradouro* overlooking the hidden valley of **Curral das Freiras** – 'one of the great sights of the world' according to H N Coleridge, nephew of the great English poet. To the east, a tract of tangled laurel forest leads to **Ribeiro Frio** ('cold river') where hikers pick up the Levada do Furado for Balções. From this vantage point – Balções means 'balconies' – one can enjoy vistas of the Ribeira da Metade valley, Faial (a *miradouro* in its own right) and the northern coast.

The coastal road from Faial to Ponta Delgada is tortuous but picturesque, skirting ravines and rounding the heads of river valleys like the spectacular **Ribeira do Pôrco** at Boaventura. Each turn in the road offers a new perspective on the scattered hamlets, littering the hillsides like broken fragments of china on a baize cloth.

ATLANTIC OCEAN

Madeira

Faial

FUNCHAL

DON'T MISS

*** Monte: Tropical Garden, Church of Our Lady of Monte, and toboggan rides.
*** Curral das Freiras: views of the 'hidden valley'.
** Câmara de Lobos: fishing village painted by Sir Winston Churchill.
** *Levada* walks: Ribeiro Frio and Pico das Pedras National Park.
** Cabo Girão: world's second highest cliff.

Opposite: *The Church of Our Lady of Monte, an important centre of pilgrimage.*

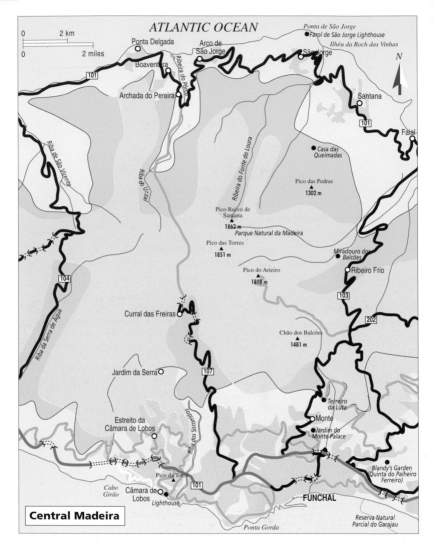

Central Madeira

The largest of these, Santana, features on every tourist itinerary but it's the walks in the Pico das Pedras National Park, rather than the celebrated thatched cottages, that linger in the memory.

CÂMARA DE LOBOS **

This famously picturesque fishing village is only 5km (3 miles) from Funchal and makes a great lunch stop. The name means 'sea wolf's lair', an allusion to the seals spotted by Zarco off the coast centuries ago. Life still revolves around the pebble beach and the adjoining boatyard, where the leathery-faced fishermen mend their nets or add an extra coat to their garishly painted boats. It's all very photogenic from the tourist's point of view but the reality is that most seamen barely make a living and are usually confined to port. At a loose end, they pass the time playing dominoes and enjoying a few glasses of *ponchas*, the local tipple made from lemon juice, honey and rum. Leave *ponchas* at least until you've had a chance to feast on grilled *espada* (scabbard fish), the speciality of the homely restaurants off the main square. *Espada* is just one of the gastronomic treats in store if you happen upon Câmara during 'Council Week' (after 29 June).

Below: *The picturesque fishing village of Câmara de Lobos.*

Beyond the boatyard some steps lead to the terrace where Sir Winston Churchill sought painterly inspiration. It took only one well-documented visit by the great statesman, in January 1950, to put Câmara de Lobos on the map.

Historians still dispute whether the **Capela de Nossa Senhora da Conceição** predates the chapel at Machico (both date from around 1420, making them the oldest religious foundations on the island). One of the primitive wall paintings in the former depicts St Nicholas delivering hard-bitten sailors from shipwreck off the Lycian coast. The parish church of **St Sebastian** is a little further up the hill and worth a quick look for the *talha dourada* (gilded wood) altarpiece, a fine example of Portuguese Baroque.

It's only a short drive from Câmara de Lobos to the *miradouro* at **Pico das Torres** (panoramic views all the way from Funchal Bay to Cabo Girâo). Follow the climbing road for just a few more kilometres and you'll reach **Estreito da Câmara de Lobos**, known for its cherries and sugar cane, but more important as a wine-growing centre. At harvest time (on or around the second week in September) there's a festival devoted to viticulture, with demonstrations, tastings, etc. If the mood takes

Right: *The Capela de Nossa Senhora da Conceição in Câmara de Lobos, founded early in the 15th century.*

you, you could make a short detour from Estreito to the scenic hamlet of **Jardim da Serra** where the celebrated 19th-century diplomat, Henry Veitch, built a *quinta* (closed to the public).

CABO GIRÃO **

You can reach this justly celebrated viewing point by road from Funchal in about 45 minutes. At 580m (1900ft), Cabo Girão is the world's second highest cliff (Norway holds the number one spot). Vertigo-inducing sea birds circle and swoop around the summit, as if daring you to follow them to the treacherous rocks below. Spare a thought for the ill-fated Henrique Alemão, whose ship came to grief there more than 500 years ago (*see* panel, page 64). Spare a thought too for the poor Madeiran farmer who has to scramble down the crumbling paths to cultivate the threadbare scraps of terrace carved from the cliff face. There's not much to keep you at the Cape apart from the souvenir stalls, the café and a small exhibition of old photographs. If you arrive reasonably early, you could take the path near the car park and walk to the attractive fishing village of **Câmara de Lobos**, arriving in time for lunch (allow about two hours). The descent is relatively easy, even for the vertically challenged, and

Above: *Houses cling precariously to the cliffs beneath Cabo Girão.*

BIRD'S-EYE VIEW

Heliatlantis offers helicopter trips over Madeira – an expensive but unforgettable way of seeing the island. There are several routes to choose from:
• A 10-minute sweep of **Funchal Bay**.
• A 15-minute overview of **Curral das Freiras**.
• A 30-minute round-trip to the east or west of the island.
• A 45-minute tour of the entire island.
Each helicopter can take up to five people at a time (prices quoted are per person).
For details, *see* 'Funchal at a Glance', page 59.

Above: *The spectacular view of Curral das Freiras from the* miradouro *at Eagle's Nest.*
Opposite: *Local handicrafts are on sale all over the island, as here at Monte.*

you'll be rewarded with views of Funchal Bay, as far as the Islas Desertas if the weather is favourable. You could pass the time trying to identify the astonishing variety of crops growing on the hillsides – everything from strawberries to potatoes.

CURRAL DAS FREIRAS ★★★

About 15km (9.3 miles) northwest of Funchal (allow at least 45 minutes if driving), this spectacular valley, enclosed by gaunt mountain peaks, is one of the island's top attractions and a 'must see'. The name Curral das Freiras means 'corral or enclosure for nuns' and dates from 1497 when João Gonçalves da Câmara gave the Santa Clara Convent sole pasture rights as an endowment – two of his daughters were novices. According to tradition, the nuns of Santa Clara took refuge here when French corsairs sacked Funchal in 1566 – the reason for the more usual translation of 'refuge' or 'hideaway'. For photographs the best vantage point is the *miradouro* at Eira do Serrado, about 450m (1476ft) above the village – at the roadside you'll see locals picking eucalyptus leaves to scent their cars. Foreign visitors have marvelled at the views since at least the 1820s when the usual mode of transport was the hammock (see panel, page 85). It was long believed that the valley was the crater of a long extinct volcano. Today most geologists favour erosion as the most likely explanation but the issue is still hotly debated. Less than 50 years ago the only way down to the village was the snaking path that starts beyond the souvenir stalls near the road tunnel. It takes a little over an hour to walk to the church from the *miradouro* and the scenery along the way is breathtaking. Curral das Freiras itself heaves with visitors, especially on Sunday (market day) when it's as brash and unsentimental as a frontier town during the gold rush. It's famous for its chestnuts – chestnut cakes, chestnut soups, even chestnut liqueur (*licor de castanha*) – and there's a chestnut festival in November. Souvenirs tend to be overpriced – household items like oven gloves, embroidered tea towels and slippers seem better value. Before you move on, take a peek at the church (no sign of nuns here nowadays) and the tiny cemetery, where photographs of the deceased adorn the tombstones.

Monte ★★★

Reaching Funchal's genteel garden suburb couldn't be easier now that the new cable car service is up and running. The eight-seater cabins take just 11 minutes to cover the 6km (3.7-mile) journey and the views of the bay on the ascent are stunning. Monte's heyday as a fashionable resort was at the end of the 19th century, when the Palace Hotel ran a sanatorium for the wealthy victims of

> **ISLAND TRAVEL**
>
> Madeirans have been ingenious in devising modes of transport specially suited to the mountainous terrain. Until the early 20th century, visitors were ferried in hammocks slung on poles and carried by two strapping men. The young Winston Churchill was fascinated by the *carro de bois*, a sledge with wooden runners, pulled by a pair of bullocks in harness (useful for negotiating Funchal's steep, cobbled streets). The Monte toboggan (*carro de cesto*) is still in service after nearly 150 years, though only as a tourist attraction. The rack-and-pinion railway that once connected **Funchal** with **Terreiro da Luta** was closed in 1939 after an engine exploded, killing four people.

LAST EMPEROR

Karl I von Habsburg was deposed as Emperor of Austria-Hungary in November 1918, after reigning for barely two years. He and his wife chose Madeira as their place of exile after first settling in Switzerland. They were given a warm reception when they arrived in Funchal harbour, on board a British ship, in November 1921. Shortly afterwards they moved from **Reid's Hotel** to the Quinta do Monte which had been placed at their disposal by the owner, a Portuguese aristocrat. Karl died in April 1922, aged 35, after succumbing to a bout of pneumonia. Many Roman Catholics came to regard him as a saint and his canonization was formally proposed in 1949.

tuberculosis. It's now a private home but the grounds are open to the public as the **Tropical Garden** (Caminho do Monte), a 7ha (17-acre) horticultural theme park with more than 100,000 plants from around the world, including 60 varieties of cycad. This ancient fern-like plant probably originated in Egypt but was in this case introduced from South Africa, where the present owner of the estate, José Berardo, made his fortune. Berardo's landscape gardeners were given free rein to create a wonderland of grottoes, spouting fountains, ornamental bridges, pagodas, streams and ponds stocked with Chinese koi fish. If this sounds a bit over the top, the **Municipal Garden** (Jardim do Monte Palace) near the town square is the perfect antidote, and it's free. The Tropical Garden is open Monday–Friday 09:00–17:00.

When the spotlights are turned on the twin-towered **Church of Our Lady of Monte**, it becomes a landmark visible from Funchal itself. A chapel was founded on this site by the first Madeirans to be born on the island (appropriately named Adam and Eve). The present building dates from the early 19th century.

Every year on the Feast of the Assumption (15 August) a medieval statue of the Virgin, said to have miraculous powers, becomes a focus for worshippers from around the island. They climb the 74 steps leading

Left: *The Monte toboggan, a mode of transport unique to Madeira.*
Opposite: *The Tropical Garden at Monte was conceived as a flight of fancy.*

to the church on their hands and knees as a mark of devotion. The marble chapel in the grounds is the last resting place of the former emperor of Austria-Hungary, Karl von Habsburg (*see* panel, page 86).

Today Monte's main claim to fame is the **toboggan** (*carro de cesto*) – actually a wicker basket on metal runners, steered and propelled (where necessary) by able-bodied men of all ages and sizes, kitted out like gondoliers. The bumpy ride down to Funchal takes about 20 minutes (you can get out halfway if you wish.) It's a unique experience, though whether it's as exhilarating as the tourist brochures make out is a matter of opinion. Bear in mind, when considering the cost, that you will need to include a tip.

If you don't want to go directly back to town, take the eucalyptus-lined road up to **Terreiro da Luta**, a noted beauty spot about 300m (984ft) above Monte. The funicular railway that used to run to here was abandoned in the 1930s – the station has been refashioned as a restaurant. After admiring the views, take a look at the monumental statue of **Our Lady of Peace**. It was erected in 1927 at the instigation of a local priest, who had lived through the bombardment of Funchal during

---

LEVADA WALKING

Do's and Don'ts:
• Take some or all of the following: high-factor sun lotion, sunglasses, a hat or cap; a warm jumper; strong, comfortable shoes with a good grip, a rainproof jacket, a pair of woollen socks, a camera, binoculars.
• Never set out without checking the weather and the state of the tracks and mountain passes.
• Never walk alone.
• Take a detailed, up-to-date map with you.
• Bring a torch if there are tunnels to negotiate.
• Have a few written phrases in Portuguese handy in case you have to ask for directions.
• Be realistic: if you suffer from vertigo, bad back, etc., avoid walks which are too challenging.
• Start with an easy walk like **Balçoes** or go with a group or tour party.
• Buy a copy of John and Pat Underwood's *Landscapes of Madeira* (Sunflower Books), available in tourist offices.

Right: *Statue of Our Lady of Peace at Terreiro da Luta, a lasting reminder of World War I.*
Opposite: *Rainbow trout thrive in the fresh mountain spring water of Ribeiro Frio.*

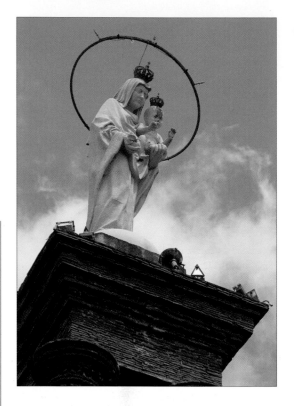

World War I – the links in the rosary were forged from the anchor chains of Allied ships. The violet, pride of Madeira, flowers around the massive basalt base between May and July.

RIBEIRO FRIO **

Picturesque Ribeiro Frio ('cold river') is a densely wooded location, popular with hikers and birdwatchers – bring binoculars if you have them. Follow the road to the spring-fed **trout hatchery**, a handy source of supply for the local restaurant. While you contemplate lunch, you can enjoy the informal **Botanical Garden**, planted exclusively with indigenous species like Madeira cedar, lily of the valley, buckthorn, cherry laurel, pride of

Madeira and yellow foxglove. The most well-trodden of the many walks in the area follows the **Levada do Furado**, signposted a little way beyond the restaurant. In one direction, it's a 30-minute stroll to the observation point of **Miradouro dos Balcões** ('balconies'). Keen-eyed ornithologists have spotted buzzards, plain swifts, grey wagtails, blackcaps, firecrests and the endemic *Columba trocaz* (long-toed pigeon) in the area, and what you don't see you'll be able to hear. From the 'balconies' there are sweeping views of the **Ribeira da Metade valley** as far as the tooth-like outcrop known as Eagle's Nest (Penha de Águia). Sir Winston Churchill captured this striking landscape in watercolour on one of his visits in the 1950s.

If you are feeling energetic, take the path in the opposite direction to the water house at **Lamaceiros**, where it joins the smaller **Levada do Portela**. Allow about three hours for this walk. It's not particularly taxing but you'll need shoes with a good grip, as the path is slippery in places and there are small streams to ford. You'll also need a good head for heights rounding the precipitous slopes of Pico do Suna and crossing the narrow ledge

carved from the rock face at Cabeço Furado. Stupendous views open up across the Ribeiro Frio valley towards the jagged crown of Pico das Torres in the west and São Roque do Faial and the peninsula of Porto da Cruz in the north. Along the way you'll see the remnants of the primitive laurel forest which once covered the island and some of the more than 70 varieties of fern which flourish in the humid microclimate.

KILLER DISEASE

Tuberculosis, or consumption as it was more commonly known before the 20th century, was at one time the single largest cause of death in the western world. Doctors were divided as to the treatment of the dreaded wasting disease but there was general agreement that a warm, dry climate was beneficial. Egypt, the French Riviera and Madeira became the favourite winter destinations of the unfortunate invalids and their companions. Those who could afford to, rented *quintas* for the season until the opening of the sanatorium at the **Monte Palace Hotel** at the end of the 19th century.

Below: *At 1861m (6108ft) Pico Ruivo de Santana (Red Peak) is Madeira's highest mountain.*

PICO DO ARIEIRO

It may come as a surprise to discover that you can drive to the summit of Madeira's third highest mountain – take the EN103 from Faial, then the EN202. The peak itself is often hidden until you emerge from the cloud drifting over the purplish moorland to bask in brilliant sunshine. From the observation point near the car park, the misty valley below Pico do Arieiro can resemble a steaming cauldron. Many first-time visitors are so impressed by the stupendous volcanic landscape that they return again and again, staying overnight in the government-run *pousada* (open during summer only – contact the tourist office in Funchal for details). To watch nature's light show as the sun rises over the peaks, bathing them in violet or vermilion hues, is an unforgettable experience. Mists descend regularly to obscure, even obliterate, views, so it's advisable to make an early start if you intend walking the four-hour return trip to **Pico Ruivo de Santana**, the highest point on the island at 1861m (6108ft). The path is well trodden but you'll need strong shoes, warm clothing and probably some nourishment – there's a café at Pico do Arieiro. When the visibility is good, the jagged panorama of knife-edge ridges, rift valleys and ravines almost takes your breath away. Lord of all you survey, you will find it difficult to conceive of the sun-drenched terraces and fertile coastline far below.

FAIAL

This lovely stretch of coastline is noted for its views, especially from the spectacular rock known misleadingly as **Penha de Águia** ('Eagle's Nest' – but there are no eagles on Madeira). The A Chave restaurant near the church serves a good lunch of *Bacalhau na Brassa* (salted cod), *Truta no forno* (baked trout) and other Portuguese specialities. The new bridge over the Ribeira Seca opened in 1980 after its predecessor was washed away by flood water – evidence that the name 'Dry River' can be dangerously misleading. If you happen to be in this unassuming hamlet during February, look out for the festival celebrating the custard apple, one of many subtropical fruits that thrive on the island.

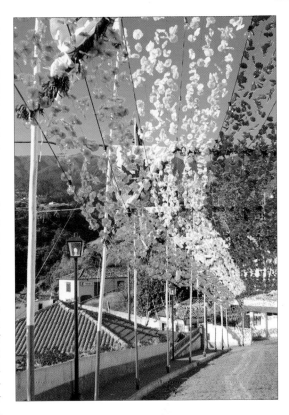

Above: *Paper flower decorations are a feature of many Madeiran festivals as seen here at Faial.*

SANTANA **

The hillside village of Santana is famous for its quaint *palheiros* – distinctive, triangular-shaped cottages with steep gables and thickly thatched roofs that all but reach the ground. In days gone by the upper storey was used as an attic for storing grain or other crops. Many of the

Above: *Pretty as a picture: thatched houses at Santana.*

houses have suffered an ignominious fate and now serve as cowsheds; the roofs made from corrugated iron rather than thatch. Surrounded by orchards and market gardens, those that have survived make an appealing subject for a photograph, especially if you can find one with washing hanging out to dry! Santana really lets its hair down for the 24 hours of the regional folk dancing festival early in September (check with the tourist office in Funchal for details).

Santana is the starting point for several scenic rambles. The easiest is no more than a gentle 5km (3-mile) stroll through the **Pico das Pedras National Park** to the government rest house at **Casa das Queimadas** where there's a picnic site. From here there's a signposted track through a beech and oak wood to **Pico das Pedras**; allow about 90 minutes, there and back. The alternative route along the **Levada do Caldeirão** is more demanding, though well worth the effort (the round trip takes about four hours).

This 11km (7-mile) hike passes through thick virgin forest of evergreen laurel and heath trees before crossing two magnificent ravines – the Ribeira dos Cedros and the Ribeira da Fonte do Louro, where emerald mosses and lichens cling to the rock face. The highlight is the point where the Ribeira Grande drops 300m (984ft) into the lagoon known as the 'Green Cauldron' (Caldeirão Verde). Bear in mind that the path has fallen away in places, making the going slippery underfoot. You'll need a torch as there are four short tunnels to negotiate.

The superb coastal walk from Santana to the village of **São Jorge** takes about two and three-quarter hours one way. The relatively open landscape at the start won't prepare you for the dramatic 250m (820ft) descent beyond the rise known as Cabaço da Vigia. At the foot of the cliff, near the abandoned settlement of Calhau, there's a separate path up to São Jorge's celebrated parish church. This walk should not be attempted in wet or windy weather.

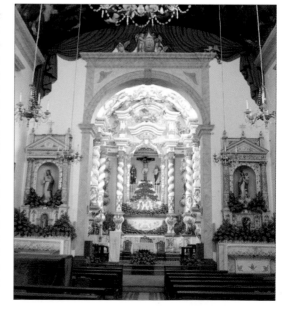

Below, *Ponta Delgada's church was rebuilt after a devastating fire in 1908.*

ARCO DO SÃO JORGE

This tiny fishing hamlet lies at the foot of a cliff. The curving coastal ridge which gives it its name is not nearly as remarkable as the gorge of the Ribeira do Pôrco, which forces the EN101 to make a tortuous detour around the valley to the cliff-top village of **Boaventura** ('Good Luck'). There's little to detain the visitor here, though there are wonderful views from the *miradouro* above the village, and there's a pleasant walk to **Archada do Pereira**, starting from the church (one and a quarter hours for the round trip).

From Boaventura the main road heads west towards **Ponta Delgada** where, once again, there are outstanding views of the village – a scattering of red-roofed houses over a promontory etched with lush, green terracing. From this vantage point you'll have no problem spotting the swimming pool on the beach, within shouting distance of the waves which pound the basalt shoreline remorselessly. On the first Sunday in September the parish of Senhor Bom Jesus (The Good Lord Jesus) celebrates one of the most important religious festivals on the island, a favourite with Madeiran emigrants who often return at this time of year. The focus of the annual pilgrimage is a wooden crucifix which, according to tradition, was washed ashore in the 16th century. Both crucifix and church were badly damaged by fire in 1908 but the charred cross is still carried in procession on the Feast of Jesus and the Holy Sacrament. (For the rest of the year it's preserved behind glass near the west door.)

The church is also the main attraction in the village of **São Jorge** on the opposite side of the bay. The lavish interior dates from the mid-18th century and is the finest example of Baroque *talha dourada* (gilded wood-carving) outside Funchal.

Below: *The altarpiece in the church at São Jorge, a splendid example of* talha dourada.

Central Madeira at a Glance

BEST TIMES TO VISIT

August–November are best for festivals: Chestnuts, Curral das Freiras, early November. Grape harvest, Câmara de Lobos, 1st half of September. Feast of the Assumption, Monte, 14th/15th August. Feast of Jesus and the Holy Sacrament, Ponta Delgada, 1st week of September.

GETTING THERE

Buses leave Funchal for Cabo Girão, Câmara de Lobos, Curral das Freiras (Eire), Faial, Monte, Ribeiro Frio and Santana.
There is a **cable car** service linking Funchal (Campo Almirante Reis) with Monte (Largo das Babosas). Hours: winter 08:30–18:30, summer 08:30–20:30; tel: 291 780 280, fax: 291 780 281.
The **Monte toboggan** (*Carreiros do Monte*) leaves from the main square, Sítio da Igreja, tel: 291 783 919.

GETTING AROUND

The easiest way is to hire a car or taxi. Bus services, while reliable, are infrequent.

WHERE TO STAY

MID-RANGE
Pousada do Pico Arieiro, Pico do Arieiro, tel: 291 230 110, fax: 291 228 611. This guesthouse on the upper slopes of Madeira's 3rd highest mountain has been a favourite with walkers for many years.

Pousada dos Vinháticos, Serra de Agua, tel: 291 952 344, fax: 291 952 540. Small guesthouse with basic facilities including restaurant and great scenery.

BUDGET
O Escondidino das Canas, Pico António Fernandes, Santana, tel: 291 572 319. A traditional Santana cottage with enough room for just four people.
O Rancho Madeirense, Pico das Pedras, Santana, tel: 291 570 230, fax: 291 572 222. These chalets make an excellent base when walking in the national park.

WHERE TO EAT

LUXURY
Quinta do Furão, Achada do Gramacho, tel: 291 570 150. Hotel-restaurant owned by the Madeira Wine Company; local wines rate higher than the food.

MID-RANGE
Churchill's Place, Câmara de Lobos, tel: 291 944 336. Pricey, but the salads and grills are above average.
Santo António, Estreito da Câmara de Lobos, tel: 291 910 360. This large touristy restaurant, specializing in *espetada*, might serve if you're driving in the area.
Victor's Bar, Ribeiro Frio, tel: 291 575 898. Handy if you're about to embark on the local *levada* walk; this friendly

eatery specializes in trout (caught in the local stream).

TOURS AND EXCURSIONS

Turivema, (Turismo Verde e Ecológico da Madeira), Edifício Baía, Loja 1 R/C Bloco Leste, Estrada Monumental 187, tel: 291 766 109, fax: 291 766 210.
Heliatlantis offers bird's-eye tours of Funchal and the island by helicopter. Tel: 291 232 882, fax: 291 232 804, or go to Estrada do Pontinha (Cais dos Contentores), between the marina and the harbour.
RR Tours, rua Dr Pita 1A, Funchal, tel: 291 982 046 or 962 986 494. Jeep safaris.
Terras de Aventura e Turismo, Caminho do Amparo 25, Funchal, tel: 291 776 818, Fax: 291 771 018.
Aeroclube da Madeira, rua do Castanheiro E2 9000-018 Funchal, tel: 291 228 311 or 964 092 580, fax: 291 221 265. Hang-gliding and para-gliding.
Mountain Bike Hire: Eurofun, *see* page 59.
Diving: Clube Naval do Seixal, *see* page 77.

USEFUL CONTACTS

Tourist Offices:
Câmara de Lobos, Largo da República, tel: 291 943 470. Open Monday–Friday 09:00–12:30, 14:00–17:30.
Santana, Sítio do Serrado, tel: 291 572 992. Open Monday–Friday 09:00–12:30, 14:00–17:30, Saturday 09:30–12:00.

5
Eastern Madeira

After Funchal, Eastern Madeira is the most densely populated part of the island. German developers began the transformation of the southern coastline between **Garajau** and **Santa Cruz** more than a decade ago. Today luxury hotels, holiday apartments, bungalows and suburban villas clutter the rocky hillsides, encouraging the traditional farming and fishing communities that eke out a living here to look to tourism as an alternative source of income. Outdoor activities are the speciality of **Caniço de Baixo**, the liveliest of these new resorts. Scuba diving is especially popular in the waters of the maritime national park at **Garajau**, but sailing, sea-fishing, tennis and golf (the **Quinta do Palheiro** course is only a 15-minute drive from **Caniço**) are all to hand. There's a lot more to the region than sport, however. The green and pleasant land of **Santo da Serra**, which incidentally boasts the island's other championship golf course, is gently wooded and excellent walking country. So too is **Portela**, where you can follow the route of the *borracheiros* (wine porters) over the mountain passes towards Funchal. One of Madeira's traditional handicrafts, wickerwork, is showcased in **Camacha**. The island's second largest town, **Machico**, is where Zarco first landed in the 15th century. The pace of life is slower here than in Funchal, but there's a beach of sorts, watersports facilities and a few hotels – just about enough for it to qualify as a resort in its own right.

After checking out the churches and the old fort, there will still be time to explore the lush **Machico valley** and

ATLANTIC OCEAN

Madeira

Machico

FUNCHAL

DON'T MISS

*** **Quinta do Palheiro Ferreiro:** magnificent subtropical gardens.
*** **Ponta de São Lourenço:** take a walk to the end of the island.
** **Camacha:** home of wickerwork.
** **Machico:** largest resort after Funchal.
* **Caniço:** swimming and scuba diving.

Opposite: *The sheltered harbour at Machico where Zarco landed in 1420.*

GOLF

Both Madeira's golf courses enjoy superb locations and unbeatable scenery. **Palheiro Golf**, designed by Cabell Robinson in 1993, is 6015m (6578 yards) long and par 71. **Santo da Serra Golf Club** opened in 1991 and first hosted the Madeira Open two years later. Designed by the American golf architect, Robert Trent Jones, it's 6039m (6604 yards) and par 72. Golfing equipment, including buggies, can be hired from the clubhouses, and professional tuition is available. Palheiro's facilities also include a putting green, covered training area and driving nets. A number of hotels offer discounts on course fees. For more information tel: 291 792 116 (Palheiro) or 291 550 100 (Santo da Serra); or consult the website: www.madeira-golf.com

the cliffs at **Pico do Facho**, from where there are commanding views towards the unspoilt eastern tip of the island at **Ponta de São Lourenço**.

Quinta do Palheiro Ferreiro ***

Within easy reach of Funchal, the magnificent gardens of Palheiro Ferreiro should feature on every tourist's itinerary. The *quinta* or villa (now a luxury hotel) was built for the Conde de Carvahal in 1804 and formed the centrepiece of an impressive country estate. The count's improvident descendants neglected the property but in 1885 it was saved from ruin by the wine exporter, John Blandy, who built a new mansion nearby (still the family home). The original garden was laid out in the French style: the ornamental ponds at the front of the old house and the stately avenue of plane trees and lofty camellias survive from this period. It was Blandy and his successors who introduced elements of the traditional English landscaped garden; hence the beeches, oaks and chestnuts, the herbaceous borders planted with delphiniums and day lilies, the immaculate lawns and neatly trimmed hedges. Essentially, though, Palheiro Ferreiro is a typically Madeiran subtropical garden, exemplified by the luxuriant *Jardim da Senhora* (Ladies' Garden) where the variety and sheer abundance of plants, shrubs and

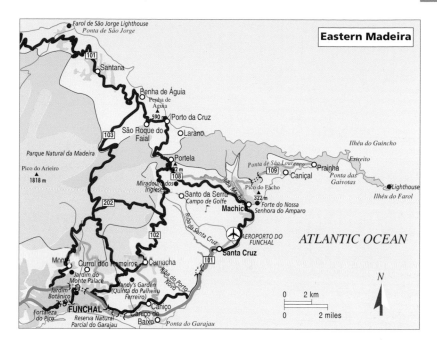

flowering trees takes the breath away: Chinese davidia, candelabra trees from Brazil, Australian jasmine, South African eaglewood, Peruvian daffodils, Madeiran geraniums and strelitzia (blood lilies) are all represented here. Elsewhere on the estate you'll see Malaysian buddleia, giant Araucaria trees, Australian banksias and (near the Baroque chapel built for the count), the crimson-flowered waratah, emblem of New South Wales. To the rear of the old house, a path leads to the sinisterly named Ribeiro do Inferno, or Hell's River. This turns out to be nothing more menacing than a damp, rather gloomy wood planted with primitive tree ferns – watch your footing as you walk.

The remainder of the Palheiro Ferreiro estate has been re-landscaped to create one of Madeira's two championship **golf courses**, with views over Funchal Bay calculated to distract the most single-minded low handicapper (*see* panel, page 98).

Opposite: *In times gone by Pico do Facho (Torch Peak) was a lookout for pirates and would-be invaders.*

Right: *Visitors enjoying a scenic stretch of the Levada dos Tornos.*
Opposite: *Hand-woven baskets are on sale in the O Relógio shop in Camacha.*

Levada dos Tornos

Madeira's longest watercourse, which is over 100km (62 miles) long, was constructed in the 1960s to supply the power station at Fajã do Nogueira. From its source, the Ribeiro São Jorge, the *levada* is tunneled under the peaks of the central mountain range to emerge just north of Monte. There's a scenic stretch beginning near Curral dos Romeiros and continuing for about 11km (7 miles) all the way to Camacha (allow 3½ hours); alternatively, leave the *levada* at **Palheiro Ferreiro** to visit the stunning gardens.

CAMACHA **

Attractively situated on a plateau surrounded by thick woodland and lush hillside terraces, Camacha is the centre of the island's wicker-weaving industry. The craft has a long pedigree – the builders of the first *levadas* used cane baskets, known as *barreleiros*, to carry tools, to clear debris, even to hoist themselves up the cliff face. Credit for turning the cottage industry into big business is usually given to a local mill owner, William Hinton. (Hinton's son, Harry, organized the first game of soccer in Camacha, years before the sport reached the Portuguese mainland – *see* panel, page 57.) In the mid-19th century

Hinton's artisans set to work imitating the cane furniture then fashionable in England and selling it to local hoteliers. Soon demand was outstripping supply as markets were found across the globe. Madeiran wickerwork is still exported to the United States, Canada, South Africa and the countries of Western Europe.

Wicker is harvested from the willow trees that thrive in the damp, humid valleys around Boaventura, where most of the plantations are located. The long, satiny shoots are soaked in water until they are supple enough to be separated from the bark. The willow is then gathered into sheaves and taken to Camacha where the workers boil the cane to make it pliable enough to fashion. The craftsmen give regular displays in **O Relógio** (The Clock), the warehouse on the main square. Both clock and bell on the tower of this former *quinta* were presented by Dr Michael Grabham, a local naturalist, in 1896 (they originally belonged to Walton parish church in Liverpool). An obsessive collector, Grabham also donated the clock on the tower of Funchal Cathedral. Every available space in the showroom is taken up by flower baskets, picnic hampers, hats, bottle holders, furniture, trays and kitchen utensils – more than 1200 items in all. (The ingenuity of the artisans would seem to be inexhaustible.) Unfortunately the wicker dogs, deer, sheep, elephants, etc., some of which took more than six months to fashion, belong to an exhibition and aren't for sale.

Camacha is also home to the Grupo Folclórico da Camacha (*see* panel), an internationally acclaimed song and dance troupe.

SANTO DA SERRA

Only a 15-minute drive from Machico, Santo da Serra (Santo António da Serra, to give the village its

---

GRUPO FOLCLORICO DA CAMACHA

Camacha's famous folk ensemble owed its early success to the efforts of its founding director, Carlos Maria dos Santos. Dr Santos assiduously researched the traditional songs and dances of the archipelago, and his enthusiasm inspired other musicians on the island. Over the years the troupe have performed at international festivals all over the world, from Holland and Estonia to Venezuela, South Africa and the United States. They spend most of their time at home, however, performing for tourists or appearing at local festivals, singing competitions, even sporting events. They've also made several recordings, available on tape or CD.

full name) enjoys a spectacular setting almost 700m (2296ft) above sea level. It was the views of the coastline around **Ponta de São Lourenço** that inspired many of Madeira's wealthier British residents to build summer retreats here in the 19th century – some of these *quintas* have since been converted to holiday lets. Farmers bring their produce to market at the weekends – the stalls line the roadside leading into the village. Near the main square is the entrance to the **Quinta do Santo da Serra**. The villa, which once belonged to the Blandy's, is closed to the public, but in the grounds there is a children's playground, a tennis court and an animal enclosure with roaming deer, goats, wild ponies and the like. Head round to the back of the estate and you'll come to a belvedere known as the **Miradouro dos Ingleses**.

The 27-hole championship **golf course** just outside the village (*see* panel, page 98) was designed by American golf architect, Robert Trent Jones, who fully exploited the natural features of the landscape and the dramatic location overlooking the Atlantic. Every spring Santo da Serra hosts the Madeira Open, now a major tournament and the first leg of the European PGA tour.

PORTELA

Driving towards Porto da Cruz, either from Funchal or Machico, it would be easy to miss Portela altogether, as it scarcely classifies as a hamlet. However, it's worth getting out of the car to stretch the legs for a few minutes, if only to admire the coastal views – **Penha de Águia** is the most obvious landmark. It can be fairly bleak when the wind gets up, but warmth and sustenance are close at hand. The homely Casa de Portela restaurant rustles up an excellent *espetada* (beef kebab), which goes down a treat with cider or local wine. Once rested, you may feel ready for a little walking. If so, pick up the **Levada do Portela** here, heading in the direction of the **Lamaceiros water house**. In good weather, this steady climb offers glorious views of Porto da Cruz and the neighbouring coastline. The **Levada do Serra do Faial** and the **Levado do**

Furado (*see* page 89) meet at Lamaceiros. The former is one of the most popular hiking trails on Madeira, and you don't need to cover all 30km (18.6 miles) of this woodland walk to appreciate its scenic beauty.

Above: *The rugged landscape from Portela to Porto da Cruz, dominated by the Penha de Águia rock.*

Opposite: *Santo da Serra golf course enjoys one of the most magnificent settings in Europe.*

PORTO DA CRUZ

According to local tradition, it was the companions of naval captain Tristão Vaz Teixeira who gave this rather desolate coastal village its name by planting a cross on the shore. Porto da Cruz grew rich on the profits of the sugar trade in the 16th century. Though the plantations have long disappeared, one of the mills has survived as a distillery, turning out a potent rum-based *aguardente* (firewater). However, it's the wine harvest that is celebrated during the first week in September with a lively procession and general knees-up. In days gone by the porters (*borracheiros*) would tramp over the Portela pass to Funchal, toting goatskins crammed with ripened grapes. You can follow in their footsteps by picking up the trail near the village bus stop, heading towards Serrado and Cruz da Guarda. It's uphill more or less all the way to the **Casa de Portela** restaurant so give your-

Right: *Statue of Christ the King overlooking Ponta do Garajau.*
Opposite: *The village of Garajau nestles at the foot of a cliff.*

self at least two hours and wear shoes with a good grip. The rugged landscape is dominated by the brooding **Penha de Águia** rock that casts a sombre shadow over the village. For a less oppressive perspective, take the cliff-top path in the opposite direction as far as **Larano**, from where there are outstanding coastal views.

Ponta do Garajau

It was the island's first settlers who noticed flocks of terns (*garajaus*) nesting in the crevices of this formidable headland just south of Caniço. Centuries later – in 1927 to be precise – a statue of Christ the King (Cristo Rei) was erected on the point, recalling a similar though much larger monument above Rio de Janeiro. A pathway leads from the summit to the foot of the cliffs and a string of rocky coves and inlets. The shoreline from Lazareto Quay in the west to Ponta da Oliveira in the east – 376ha (929 acres) in all – has been designated a nature reserve (Reserva Natural Parcial do Garajau). Conservation measures are in force here to protect the marine species that thrive in the coastal waters: groupers, moray eels, barracudas, parrot fish, trigger fish and manta rays.

CANIÇO *

Caniço's strategic location between Funchal and the airport has led to it becoming one of the fastest developing tourist resorts on the island, with villas, bungalows, aparthotels and entertainment complexes encroaching from every direction. The village itself is situated a little way inland and is dominated by its church, a handsome building, easily distinguished by its slender campanile. Much older is the Chapel of the Mother of God at **Mãe de Deus**, founded in 1536 and with its original portal and a few other Manueline features still intact. Caniço is well served with bars and restaurants, although the majority of visitors spend more time in **Caniço de Baixo**, about 2km (1.2 miles) away at the foot of the cliff. Amenities include a mini-market as well as cafés and other eateries to the rear of the stony beach. The golf course at Palheiro is only twenty minutes' drive away and there are diving clubs at the Roca Mar Hotel and the Lido Hotel Galomar (PADI affiliated), where beginners, including children, are welcome and four- or five-day training courses are available. Scuba diving is the ideal way to enjoy the protected waters of the **Garajau natural marine park** (*see* panel, page 112).

SCUBA DIVING CENTRES

The most rewarding area for scuba diving is around Caniço de Baixo and Machico. Equipment can be hired from the companies listed below, but you'll need a log book, diving certificate and possibly medical certificate. Most firms also offer courses for beginners with equipment provided.
Manta Diving Centre, Lido Hotel Galomar, Caniço de Baixo, tel: 291 934 566, fax: 291 934 555.
Atalaia Club, Hotel Roca Mar, Caniço, tel: 291 934 330, fax: 291 933 011.
Hotel Dom Pedro Baia, Machico, tel: 291 967 435, fax: 291 966 889.
See also pages 59 and 113.

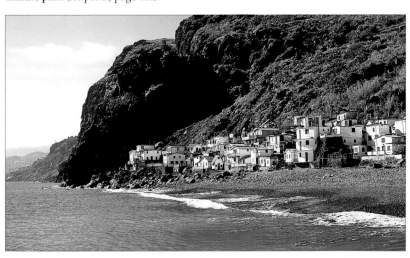

GAME FISHING

A number of firms offer deep-sea fishing trips off the coast of Madeira. Prices include the hire of equipment.
In Funchal, contact:
Katherine B, Captain Peter Bristow, Quinta das Malvas, rua de Santa Luzia 124, tel: 291 220 334.
In Caniço:
Missiltour, vista do Mar 4, Garajau, tel: 291 933 414.
In Machico:
Nautileste, Largo da Praça, tel: 291 965 248.
See also panel on page 41.

Below: *Swimming pool terrace in the modern resort-village of Caniço de Baixo. The local waters form part of the Garajau natural marine park.*

SANTA CRUZ

The proximity of Madeira's recently expanded international airport hasn't proved a blight on this attractive village and holiday resort, now only about 15 minutes' drive from Funchal. Santa Cruz's parish church, dedicated to **São Salvador**, was built between 1479 and 1533 and is one of the largest and most appealing on the island. You'll be forgiven for thinking that the architecture bears more than a passing resemblance to the cathedral in Funchal – Pedro Eanes almost certainly had a hand in the design of both buildings. The exterior of the parish church lacks the ornamental detail and *azulejo* decoration of its rival in the capital, but look inside and you'll find plenty to admire: a tripartite nave, enlarged in the 17th century, splendid Gothic arches and ribbed vaulting from the Manueline period, and a commendably restrained gilded altarpiece (18th century). The **town hall** is almost as old as the church although only the pointed Gothic arches on the doors and windows of the façade have emerged unscathed from a succession of facelifts. Also look out for the **law courts** in Rua da Ponta Nova, a handsome colonial-style building dating from the 19th century, with a sweeping stone staircase, balustered verandahs and a colourful subtropical garden. Date palms and prickly dragon trees provide shade along the promenade, where you'll find seafront cafés, spotlessly clean mosaic pavements, manicured grass verges and pretty flowerbeds. The main attraction though is the Praia das Palmeiras (Palm Beach) Lido. The amenities here include a bar and restaurant, sunbeds, a paddling pool as well as sea access.

MACHICO **

For a very brief period after the discovery of Madeira, Machico – 5km (3 miles) east of Santa Cruz – was the notional capital; it's still the most important town after Funchal, though minuscule by comparison. Machico's founder, Tristão Vaz Teixeira, administered the eastern side of the island from here, while Zarco governed the west. There's a **statue of Teixeira** in the main square, Largo do Municipio – local buses and taxis depart from here. Machico's impressive parish church of **Nossa Senhora da Conceição** dates from the 15th century and retains a number of Manueline features, including the portal, rose window and slender Gothic chancel arch. Dom Manuel I of Portugal himself donated the marble columns on the side door, along with an organ and various works of art. This is not quite the oldest religious foundation in the town, however; that honour goes to the **Capela dos Milagres** (Chapel of Miracles) on Largo dos Milagres, the cobbled square with a neglected air on the far side of the river. The church was renamed when a precious medieval crucifix, washed away during a flood in 1803, was recovered by American mariners out at sea. Machico's third church is

Above: *The striking colonial architecture of Santa Cruz Law Court dates from the 19th century.*

FREE TRADE ZONE

The abolition of whaling in the early 1980s dealt a severe blow to the Madeiran economy. While a handful of whalemen were employed as advisors to the Society for the Protection of Marine Mammals, or as museum guides in **Caniçal**, the majority were forced to scrape a living from tuna fishing. To provide long-term regeneration for the area, the European Union, supported by the Portuguese and Madeiran governments, has established a Free Trade Zone, so far with mixed results.

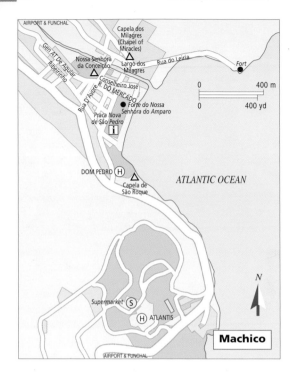

Machico

dedicated to **São Roque**. Also founded in the 15th century, it was rebuilt in 1739 with a disproportionate Baroque doorway. It's rarely open but if you can get to see inside, there are some attractive 18th-century *azulejos*. Machico once boasted not one but three fortresses, an indication of its erstwhile importance. The triangular **Forte do Nossa Senhora do Amparo** stands in a park overlooking the sea and is open to the public. It dates from 1706 and last saw some action during the Miguelite Rebellion in 1828. Through the cobbled courtyard is Machico's **tourist office**.

The gentle shelving of the stony beach makes swimming here enjoyable, even if the water isn't quite as clean as in more secluded spots along the coast. A couple of beach cafés serve up tasty local fish, with spaghetti and salads; otherwise it's the hot dog stall if you don't want to venture further inland. Water sports enthusiasts can hire skis, windsurfing boards and canoes from a number of outfits along the seafront. Sailing and fishing trips can also be arranged from here. Machico is well served with bars and restaurants, mostly concentrated around the Traversa do Mercado, the main shopping street. Machico's red-letter days come at the end of August (when there's a torchlight procession to the Chapel of Miracles) and 8–9 October (the local carnival).

The Largo dos Milagros is the starting point of an enjoyable walk to the cliffs of **Pico do Facho**. As you climb the hill, there are fine views of the town and its diminutive football stadium, but nothing to compare with the panoramic vista from the top, as the peninsula tapers towards **Ponta de São Laurenço**, the most easterly point of the island. Back in the 16th century, bonfires were lit on Pico do Facho to warn the people of Machico that a pirate attack was imminent – a vital link in the chain of coastal defences.

Follow the track down to the Caniçal tunnel entrance, continue along the main road for about 15 minutes and you'll arrive at the **Levada Nova** from where you can set out to explore the lightly wooded hillsides of the Ribeira Seca valley and the terraced fields above Machico.

ROBERT MACHIN

According to legend, the first man to set foot on Madeira was Robert Machin, an English nobleman during the reign of Edward III (1327–77). All that is known for certain about him is that he traded with the Italian cities of Genoa and Venice and that at some point he was banished from England. The chroniclers relate how he and his mistress, Anne of Hertford, were shipwrecked during a storm and eventually ended up on Madeira. Machin left Anne with the crew and set off to reconnoitre the island, but during his absence the sailors abandoned the hapless woman and her page and took flight. When Anne died three days later, Robert built a chapel over the site and was eventually buried there himself. **Zarco** found the graves and named the place Machico after Machin.

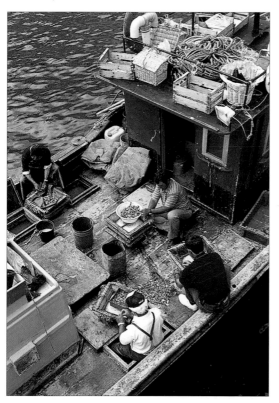

Left: *Fishing is still important to the economy of Machico.*

CANIÇAL

Back in the 1950s, this sleepy fishing village, 9km (5.6 miles) northeast of Machico, was so inextricably linked with the whaling industry that action sequences for the film *Moby Dick* were shot off the coast here (*see* panel, page 111). In those days, Caniçal was still accessible only by boat or via a precarious cliff-top path. After the international ban on whaling in 1982, the disused station re-opened as the **Museu da Baleia** (Whaling Museum). The exhibition tells the story of whale hunting on the island, mainly through charts and photographs. Visitors get to learn about the lives of the whalemen, the dangers they encountered on the high seas, their traditional hunting techniques, and the ritual celebrations that followed their safe return to port. The drama of the grim encounter between man and beast is thrown into stark relief by the weapons on display – harpoons, spears, ropes and grappling hooks – none of which could be used until the whale was almost under the boat. The life-size fibreglass model of a cachalot, or sperm whale, set alongside a typical open whaler, shows just how precarious the struggle could be and how prone the vessel was to capsize. The tour concludes with a 45-minute video (in English) which explains how marine biologists on the island now work hand in hand with the fishermen in conserving these beautiful creatures.

Opposite: *Whaling and the port of Caniçal were synonymous until the practice was banned in the 1980s.*

Below: *Street sellers in the pretty coastal village of Caniçal. Until 1982, when the practice was banned, most of the local fishermen earned their livelihood from whaling.*

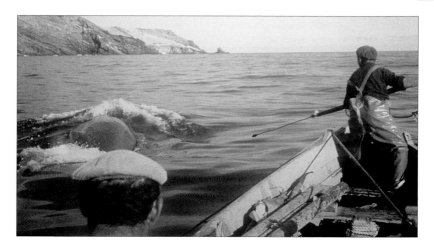

PRAINHA

A side turning off the EN101-3 east of Caniçal leads to Prainha, which has the distinction of being the only natural sand beach on the island. Porto Santo it isn't – Prainha ('little beach' in Portuguese) is barely 100m (109yd) long, the sand is gritty and the crowds can pall on a hot summer's weekend. On the plus side, there's a café-bar, showers and good swimming in and around the inlet.

Perched on the crest of a hill overlooking the beach is the **Capela de Nossa Senhora de Piedade** that was built at the expense of local fishermen in 1921. Once a year, on the third Sunday of September, a statue of the Virgin is carried in procession from the parish church in Caniçal to the shore, from where it is escorted by a flotilla of brightly decorated boats to the chapel at Prainha.

PONTA DE SÃO LOURENÇO ★★★

The most relaxing way to see Madeira's most easterly point is to take the boat trip from **Funchal** to **Ponta do Furado**, viewing **Garajau**, **Caniço de Baixo**, **Machico** and **Caniçal** en route. Alternatively, follow the EN101-3 to the car park just before Baía de Abra and walk. Bear in mind that this is quite a demanding hike and you'll need

---

MOBY DICK

Released in 1956, the film *Moby Dick* was directed by John Huston and starred Gregory Peck and Orson Welles. Only the opening sequences were shot on Madeira owing to rough weather – the crew decamped to Youghal, off the coast of Ireland, for the other whaling scenes. Ray Bradbury's screenplay was based on Herman Melville's classic tale of Captain Ahab's obsession with taking revenge on the whale that had taken off his leg on an earlier expedition. Craving authenticity Huston and Peck (though not Welles it seems), befriended the whalers of **Caniçal** who, after some persuasion, took them on a whaling expedition. Despite seasickness, both men relished the experience and returned to **Reid's Hotel** impressed with the crew's courage and strength.

Above: *Ponta de São Lourenço, the easternmost point on the island.*

DIVING SITES

Madeira's coastal waters support a rich marine life. Visibility is excellent – up to 50m (164ft) at Ponta de São Lourenço – which accounts for the growing number of scuba-diving schools. Most are based around **Caniço de Baixo,** popular due to its proximity to Machico Bay and the **Garajau** natural marine park. Here you may encounter monkfish, barracudas, octopus, sea spiders, eels, manta rays, the great locust lobster and other species that thrive in Atlantic waters. The clubs offer courses with equipment provided. Wreck and night dives are also organized.

---

to be properly equipped. Today the peninsula is almost barren, the vermilion-tinged rock reminiscent of the Martian landscape in places, but it was not always so. In the days of the first settlers the area was heavily forested but the soil never recovered once the trees were uprooted to provide more land for pasture. Each spring, however, Ponta de São Lourenço comes abruptly to life as a rash of flowers breaks out miraculously among the scrub. From the observation point below the car park you'll be able to make out land's end and the lighthouse beyond, left high and dry on its own jagged islet (**Ilhéu do Farol**). There are equally compelling views as the footpath follows the curve of the bay, notably at 'Sea Horses', a triangular rock formation off the north coast, and at 'Seagull's Peak' (at Ponta das Gaivotas), about 300m (984ft) above the pounding Atlantic Ocean. Take your binoculars to appreciate the bird life of the peninsula: terns, Cory's shearwaters, little egrets, buzzards, whimbrels, kestrels and rock doves are all regular visitors. The going gets tougher, and the terrain more vertiginous, beyond the house at Casa Sardinhas – a favourite picnic spot, where you may want to call it a day.

Eastern Madeira at a Glance

BEST TIMES TO VISIT

July–October are best for festivals: Feast of the onion, Caniço, mid-August. Gastronomy week, Machico, end July, beginning August. Carnival (Feast of the Holy Sacrament), Machico, last weekend in August. Grape harvest, Porto da Cruz, 1st week of September. Apple harvest, Santo da Serra, 1st week of September. Feast of Our Lord of Miracles, Machico, 9 October.

GETTING THERE

Buses leave Funchal for Camacha, Caniçal, Caniço, Garajau, Machico, Porto da Cruz, Santa Cruz, Santo da Serra, Quinta do Palheiro Ferreiro. To reach Prainha and São Lourenço take the bus to Caniçal, then a taxi.

GETTING AROUND

The easiest way to get around is to hire a car or taxi. Bus services, while reliable, are infrequent.

WHERE TO STAY

LUXURY

Quinta Splendida, Sítio da Vargem, Caniço, tel: 291 930 400, fax: 291 930 401. This modern hotel in the village, not the resort, occupies the grounds of an historic *quinta*.
Roca Mar, Caniço de Baixa, tel: 291 934 334. Luxury resort hotel with diving club, pools, evening entertainment, shuttle bus to Funchal, etc.

MID-RANGE

Pensão Amparo, Rua da Amargura, Machico, tel: 291 968 120, fax: 291 966 050. Small, friendly, near beach.
Dom Pedro Garajau, Garajau, tel: 291 930 800, fax: 291 930 801. Reliable, convenient for local resorts.
Estalagem do Santo, Casais Próximos, Santo António da Serra, tel: 291 552 595, fax: 291 552 596. Modern hotel with rural location, handy for Santo da Serra golf course.

WHERE TO EAT

LUXURY

Casa Velha do Palheiro, Estalagem Casa Velha do Palheiro, Palheiro Golf, São Gonçalo, tel: 291 794 901. French chef gives classic Portuguese dishes a makeover.

MID-RANGE

O Galã, Rua General António Teixeira de Aguiar, Machico, tel: 291 965 720. Brightly decorated café and patisserie, popular with locals.

BUDGET

A Nossa Aldeia, Sítio dos Casais Próximos, Santa Antonio da Serra, tel: 291 552 142. Hamburgers, *espetada*.
Hortensia Gardens, Caminho dos Pretos 89, São João Latrão, tel: 291 792 179. Tearooms on the Levada dos Tornos.
O Boléu, Camacha, tel: 291 922 128. Serves homely Madeiran meals.

O Túnel, Estrada do Caniçal, Machico, tel: 291 962 459. Pleasant roadside restaurant, just outside town.

TOURS AND EXCURSIONS

Turivema, *see* page 59.
Heliatlantis, *see* page 59.
There is a **boat excursion** from Funchal marina to Ponta de São Lourenço, with a stopover at Caniçal for lunch.
Golf: *see* panel, page 98.
Jet Ski/ Water Ski: Nautileste, Largo da Praça, Machico, tel/fax: 291 965 248.
Diving: Manta Diving Centre, Lido Hotel Galomar, Caniço de Baixo, tel: 291 934 566, fax: 291 934 555.
Atalaia Club, Hotel Roca Mar, Caniço, tel: 291 934 330.
Motorcycle and bike rental: Magos Bike, Canico de Baixo, tel: 291 934 818, fax: 291 934 819, website: magoscar.com

USEFUL CONTACTS

Tourist Offices: Caniço, Caniço de Baixo, tel: 291 932 919. Open Monday–Friday 09:30–13:00, 14:30–15:30, Saturday 09:30–12:00.
Santa Catarina Airport, tel: 291 524 933. Open Monday–Tuesday 09:00–20:00, Wednesday 09:00–00:00, Thursday–Friday 09:00–21:00, Saturday–Sunday 09:00–15:00 and 18:00–00:00.
Machico, Forte Nossa Senhora de Amparo, tel: 291 962 289. Open Monday–Friday 09:00–12:30, 14:00–17:00, Saturday 09:30–12:00.

6
Porto Santo

Just 11km (6.8 miles) long and 7km (4.3 miles) wide, the island of Porto Santo lies some 40km (25 miles) northeast of Madeira, but the landscape couldn't be more different. Madeira's satellite is more like a desert island – parched, arid and, for the most part, flat, hence the soubriquet 'tawny isle'. The 5000 inhabitants have the place to themselves for most of the year, but in August the picture changes as Madeirans and mainland Portuguese arrive in numbers for the summer vacation. The attraction is the 9km (5.6 miles) of pure golden sand extending along the southern coastline. The climate too is ideal, with very little rainfall, generous amounts of sunshine, and warm sea temperatures. Hiring a bike could be the best way to see the island, but there are also boat trips, taxi tours and a couple of hiking trails. You can climb at least two of the peaks (**Pico do Facho** and **Pico do Castelo**), while **Morenos**, the greenest spot, and **Fonte da Areia**, the island's mini-spa, are great for picnics. Bird-watchers too have a field day here – hoopoes, black-headed gulls, snipe, plovers, sandpipers, sanderlings, wagtails, pipits and rock sparrows have all been sighted.

Christopher Columbus is said to have lived on Porto Santo for a time – his house is the only real tourist site in the island capital of **Vila Baleira**.

VILA BALEIRA ★★★

There's little natural shade on the **beach** so bring plenty of sunblock and a head covering. Swimming in the warm, translucent waters is an unadulterated pleasure, the soft

ATLANTIC OCEAN

Porto Santo

Madeira

Machico

FUNCHAL

Ilhas Desertas

Opposite: *The beach at Porto Santo. Soft sand underfoot makes a welcome change from the stony shelving of Madeiran beaches.*

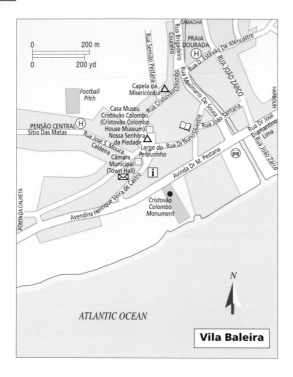

Vila Baleira

sand underfoot making a welcome change after the stony shelving of Madeiran beaches. Amenities include several cafés, showers, toilets and palm umbrellas. For a more active holiday, enquire at the tourist office for details of the diving school (beginners are welcome), the three-hour boat excursion around the island (dolphin sightings are promised), and the deep-sea fishing trips in search of blue marlin. Windsurfing, paragliding, volleyball and donkey rides are also available, depending on the weather and the season, while the larger hotels such as the Hotel Vila Baleira and the Porto Santo offer tennis courts, mini-golf and gymnasiums. At Hotel Vila Baleira there is even a thalassotherapy centre where marine products are used for therapeutic treatments.

At the heart of the tiny port of Vila Baleira is the sand-blown square, **Largo do Pelourinho**, where the unassuming whitewashed houses, dressed with pink oleander, are shaded by palms and dragon trees. The entrepreneurial-minded early settlers soon discovered that the sap from the latter, known as *sangue de drago* (dragon's blood), could be exploited commercially as a fabric dye. The Morgada chapel in the parish church of **Nossa Senhora da Piedade** dates from the time of the discoverers, anticipating Vila Baleira's **town hall** by about 100 years.

Just behind the square, on Rua Cristóvão Colombo, is the **Christopher Columbus House Museum**. While there's

CULINARY FAVOURITES

Many restaurants in **Vila Baleira** (Porto Santo) specialize in fish dishes. Stewed or roasted parrot fish is one delicacy, while the stew *fragateria*, sometimes translated as 'kettle of fish', is also worth trying. Surprisingly, given the arid landscape, Porto Santo also produces Verdelho and Malvasia wines, harvested as early as August owing to the warmth of the sun and the sandy soil. Production has been increasing in recent years.

no documentary proof that the great explorer lived here, it is certain that he visited Porto Santo in or around 1478 and that he married the daughter of Bartolomeu Perestrelo, Filipa Moniz. Anyone looking for evidence of the couple's day-to-day life here, however, will be disappointed – the small exhibition consists mainly of reproductions – charts, engravings and unauthenticated portraits. It is open Tuesday–Friday 10:00–18:00, weekends and public holidays 10:00–13:00, tel: 291 983 405.

PONTA DA CALHETA **

Beyond the *miradouro* at Ponta da Calheta, Porto Santo's seemingly infinite expanse of glistening sand finally comes to an end, giving way to a more ragged coastline of bays, coves and inlets more typical of Madeira. Set out from Vila Baleira late in the afternoon and revel in the spectacular sunsets and views of **Ilhéu de Baixo**, one of Porto Santo's island satellites. The terrace of the Pôr do Sol restaurant is a perfect place to relax over a meal of grilled fish, washed down by a bottle of local Verdelho.

FONTE DA AREIA **

To visit the springs at Fonte da Areia take the bus to Camacha and walk. The therapeutic properties of the water that seeps from Porto Santo's mineral-rich sand-

---

ENDANGERED SPECIES

Also know as the 'sea wolf' (*Lobo Marinho*), the monk seal is currently one of the five most endangered species on the planet. Apart from the **Desertas**, where there are around 20 pairs at present, the main breeding grounds are the Aegean and the north coast of Morocco. Closed-circuit television cameras have been installed on the Desertas to monitor the seals' progress. Persistent culling by fishermen led them to take refuge in caves along the coast but recently (and highly unusually) there have been seals on the beach itself, their natural habitat. There are also encouraging signs that reproduction is beginning to take off again, after several disappointing years.

Below: *The beach on Porto Santo is said to have health-giving properties.*

stone have long been known, and a long-sceptical medical profession now recognizes the benefits. Rheumatism, varicose veins, kidney ailments, eczema, even bone diseases are thought to respond to its curative properties. In the 19th century, when spa towns were the rage in Europe, drinking fountains were installed at Fonte da Areia and other strategic points across the island – you may already have tasted the mineral water, as it's widely available in Madeira's restaurants. Soak up the coastal views from the snack bar alongside the fountain, before taking a closer look at the cliffs – Fonte da Areia's other point of interest. Wind and rain erosion have created natural sculptures and weird and wonderful patterns on the soft, flaky sandstone. A path descends from the cliff top to a small pebble beach with rock pools.

A TOUR OF THE ISLAND

Vila Baleira is often referred to as Porto Santo, its original name. According to the Portuguese chronicle, *Saudades da Terra*, when the sea captains Zarco and Teixeira were washed up on the island after being blown off course during a storm, they named their place of refuge Porto Santo, meaning 'holy' or 'blessed' port.

Hire a car or a taxi and in half a day you'll be able to see most of what the island has to offer; alternatively, hire a bike or a motorcycle (don't forget your sunglasses, sunblock and water bottle).

Leave Vila Baleira on Rua Bispo de Alencastre and follow the signs to Serra de Fora. The road skirts around the Vale do Touro, passing a turnoff to the Chapel of Nossa Senhora da Graça (founded 1533), on the way to the *miradouro* at **Portela** about 2km (1.2 miles) further. The landmark here is a spindle-and-sail windmill, one of a number dotted about the island, used originally for grinding corn. The observation point affords views of the celebrated beach to the west, and of the cone-shaped Pico de Baixo and Ilhéu de Cima (complete with lighthouse) to the east.

Beyond Serra de Fora is the broad valley of the **Serra de Dentro**. The efforts of local farmers to eke out a living from

Porto Santo

Ilhéu de Fora

Baixa do Meio

Baixa dos Barbeiros

Ilhéu das Cenouras

Ilhéu da Fonte da Areia

Furnas das Amasiadas

Porto das Eira

Pedregal de Dentro

Pico da Cabeta Pico das Urzes

Porto das Salemas

Estação Lora

450 m

Cabeço da Lagoa

Serra de Dentro

440 m

Fonte da Areia Spring

Eiras Velhas

Camacha

Ponta do Varadouro

Ponta de S. Miguel

Farabo

517 m Pico do Facho

Pico do Conselho

437 m Pico do Castelo

Engue

324 m

Serra de Fora

Ponta dos Ferreiros

Furnas

Chapel o

Pico do Macfico

285 m Porto dos Frades

Lanque

Cashi

Zimbro

Salões

Portela Penedo

Pico de Baixo

206 m Pon. Galé

Campo de Cima

Vila Baleira

(Porto Santo)

Port de Abrigo

Pedras Pretas

Fontina

Ilhéu de Cima

Espinto Santo

Campo de Baixo

ATLANTIC OCEAN

Morenos Pienin Site

Pico do Ana Ferreira

283 m

Ilhéu de Ferro

Ribeiros

Ponta

Ponta do Gabriel

Zimbralinho

Ponta da Calheta

Boqueirão de Baixo

N

0   2 km

0   1 mile

Ilhéu de Baixo ou da Cal

Ponta da Isabel

Eira

Ponta do Patacho

Ponta do Ilhéu

crops grown on the hillsides have been frustrated by the perennial shortage of water. Traditionally the limestone houses here were covered with the dark grey clay known as *salão*. During the summer, the clay dries and cracks appear, allowing the air to circulate, while in winter *salão* absorbs the rain like a sponge.

The Estrela do Norte (Northern Star) restaurant is the only reason to linger in the hamlet of **Camacha**. From here you could take the side road to **Fonte da Areia** (*see* page 117). Otherwise leave Camacha in the direction of **Pico do Castelo**, named for its now ruined fort which

Above: *Windmills on Porto Santo were once a familiar part of the landscape but are now a rarity.*

was built in the 16th century to defend the island against pirate attack – with little success, judging by the historical records. Pico do Castelo is a fairly arduous climb in hot weather, so don't set out without a water bottle. From here you could hike to the next hilltop, Pico do Facho, for even better views. The name, Torch Peak, is a reminder of the days when bonfires warned settlers that the corsairs were approaching. (One refuge for the fleeing population was **Furnas das Amasiadas**, a cave on the northeastern coast where the pits for storing food can still be seen.)

From Pico do Castelo, either return to Vila Baleira and call it a day, or take the beach road to the west of the town. Looking right, after a couple of minutes you'll notice the tawny-coloured mound, Pico de Ana Ferreira, named after an illegitimate daughter of Dom João II of Portugal. The road runs out at **Ponta da Calheta** (*see page 117*). Two other beauty spots could be explored from here: the secluded pebble beach at **Zimbralinho**, and **Morenos**, one of the greenest spots on the island and good for picnicking.

ILHAS DESERTAS

The 'Desert Islands' (Deserta Grande, Ilhéu Chão and Búgio) lie approximately 30km (19 miles) off the coast of Madeira, from where they are often visible. There was a time, centuries ago, when Deserta Grande was inhabited, though the barren terrain and arduous conditions soon drove the settlers away, leaving the mountain goats, rabbits and the giant, highly venomous black spider, *Lycosa ingens*, to fend for themselves. Since 1990, when the islands were claimed as a nature reserve, no one has been allowed to land without a government permit. The Desertas are not completely out of bounds, however – when sea conditions are favourable it's possible to join one of the boat excursions exploring the coastal waters. While you're unlikely to spot the monk seals, an endangered species, you will see the colonies of sea birds, including Atlantic shearwaters and petrels – the soft-plumed petrel being indigenous to these islands. For the best sightings, come between April and mid-November.

Porto Santo at a Glance

Porto Santo enjoys pretty much year-round sunshine and the temperature rarely falls below 20°C (68°F). The crowds arrive in July and disperse at the beginning of September. At other times of the year, you'll have the island more or less to yourself.

The *Lobo Marinho* (Sea wolf) **ferry** from Funchal to Porto Santo (daily except Tuesdays) takes about 2½ hours. Pre-booking is essential in July and August, although the situation may ease once the new ferry comes into operation by the end of 2003. It's also possible to reach Porto Santo by **catamaran** (1½ hours). From the port, **taxis** deliver guests to hotels, otherwise it's a short walk to the near (eastern) end of the beach. There are several **flights** daily from Funchal airport (journey time 15 minutes). Tickets can be obtained from any travel agent or branches of TAP, the Portuguese national airline. Pre-booking is essential in high season.

The easiest way is to hire a car, a taxi or even a bike.

LUXURY
Hotel Vila Baleira, Sítio do Cabeço da Ponta, Porto Santo, tel: 291 980 800, fax: 291 980 801. Brand new high-rise, four stars, with thalassotherapy centre, outdoor and indoor swimming pools and beach club.
Luamar, Cabeço da Ponta, 4km (2.5 miles) from Vila Baleira, tel: 291 984 121, fax: 291 983 100. Over 100 self-catering apartments with satellite TV, snack bar, tennis court, sauna and pool.
Porto Santo Hotel, Campo de Baixo, tel: 291 980 140, fax: 291 980 149. Renovated a few years ago, the amenities include a bar, restaurant, swimming pool, tennis court, mini-golf and windsurfing.

MID-RANGE
Mar e Sol, Campo de Baixo, tel: 291 982 269. Seafood restaurant near the Porto Santo Hotel.
Restaurante Marques, Rua João Santana, Vila Baleira, tel: 291 982 319. Standard Madeiran fare.
Pôr do Sol, Ponta da Calheta, tel: 291 984 380. Terrace restaurant serving up tasty fish dishes.

While many visitors are happy with an after-dinner stroll along the beach, there's no shortage of night-time entertainment in Vila Baleira. **Zarco Bar** (tel: 291 982 046) and **Mercenaria**, both on Rua Zarco, are lively venues, as is the beach café, **Tia Maria**. The restaurant and bar of the La Roca Yacht Club has a verandah overlooking the sea. **Quinta do Serrado** offers live music every evening while the **Porto Santo Hotel** is a venue for jazz. There are currently two discos on the island: **Challenger**, Rua D. Esteva de Alencastre, and **Big Boy**, Rua João Santana. **Club Naval do Porto Santo**, 9400 Porto Santo, tel: 291 985 190, fax: 291 982 585. Boat and canoe trips. **URS Moser**, rua João Gonçalves Zarco 5, Porto Santo, tel: 291 982 162, fax: 291 982 163. Diving, boat trips and scooter rentals. **Motorbike and cycle rental:** Autoacessórios Colombo Avenida Henrique Veira de Castro, Porto Santo, tel: 291 984 458.

Porto Santo Line, rua da Praia 4, Funchal, tel: 291 210 300, fax: 291 226 434.
TAP Air Portugal, Avenida das Comunidades Madeirenses 10, Funchal.
Porto Santo Airport, tel: 291 982 925.
Tourist Office, Avenida Henrique Veira e Castro 5, Vila Baleira, tel: 291 982 361. Open Monday–Friday 09:00–17:30, Saturday 10:00–12:30.
Post Office, Avenida Henrique Veira de Castro, tel: 291 980 011.
Police, tel: 291 982 423.
Emergency Surgery, tel: 291 980 060.

Travel Tips

Tourist Information

Canada, 60 Bloor Street West, Suite 1005, Toronto, Ontario, M4W 3B8, tel: 416 921 7376, fax: 416 921 1353. 500 Sherbrooke Street West, Suite 940, Montreal, Quebec, H3A 3C6, tel: 514 282 1264, fax: 514 499 1450.

Portugal, Lisboa Welcome Centre, Praça do Comércio, Lisbon, tel: 21 031 2810.

South Africa, 4th Floor, Sunnyside Ridge, Sunnyside Drive, Parktown, 2193 Johannesburg, tel: 2711 484 3487, fax: 2711 484 5416.

UK, Portuguese National Tourist Office, 22–25a Sackville Street, London W1X 1DE, tel: 0906 364 0610, fax: 020 7494 1868.

USA, Portuguese National Tourist Office, 590 Fifth Avenue, 4th Floor, New York, NY 10036–4702, tel: 212 354 4403, fax: 212 764 6137.

Funchal Tourist Office, Avenida Arriaga 18, tel: 291 229 057, fax: 291 232 151. See 'At a Glance' pages for offices in other areas.

Entry Requirements

Every visitor must be in possession of a valid passport. Citizens of European Union countries, Canada, the United States of America or Japan do not require a visa; other nationalities should contact their Portuguese consulate for all stays of up to 90 days.

Customs

Portugal, as a member of the European Union, is subject to its customs regulations. Limits are imposed on goods obtained duty free within the EU and on goods bought outside the EU. Other items bought within the EU are governed by 'guidance levels' which recommend amounts considered to be for personal use. Narcotics, firearms and other weapons, obscene material and unlicensed animals are all prohibited.

Health Requirements

No special immunizations are required, or necessary. There is no free health service on Madeira, so it is recommended that you take out medical insurance to cover emergencies. Make sure you keep receipts if you intend to make a claim. EU citizens should fill in form E111 that enables them to claim a refund on basic healthcare.

Air Travel

Santa Catarina airport handles flights from most European destinations, either direct or via Lisbon. The flight time is about 4 hours from London. As flying is the only way to enter Madeira, most flights are fully booked, especially during the summer. The airport is 22km (14 miles) from the capital, Funchal – 50 minutes by bus (irregular service), 35 minutes by taxi. TAP Air Portugal (Funchal), tel : 291 235 185, fax: 291 239 265.

What to Take

Take clothing that covers all eventualities. In the summer, dress for hot weather with a jacket or jumper for evenings. Always take something waterproof – it may rain at any time. If you are planning to walk along a *levada* or in the mountains you will need stout shoes or walking boots. Don't forget a sun hat, sun cream, water bottle and a camera.

Money Matters

Euro bank notes and coins were introduced into Portugal on 1 January 2002 to replace the Portuguese currency, the escudo. Exchange rates for visitors from outside the euro zone are clearly displayed in banks, currency exchange offices and hotels.

Coins are issued in denominations of 1, 2, 5, 10, 20 and 50 euro cents and 1 and 2 euros. Notes are issued in denominations of 5, 10, 20, 50, 100, 200 and 500 euros.

All major credit cards and traveller's cheques are widely accepted in shops, restaurants and hotels. Banks and ATM cashpoints can be found in Funchal and the larger towns across the island. Tipping is not generally expected on Madeira and most hotels and restaurant bills include service as well as IVA (VAT). A small tip (10%) for good service can be left at your discretion.

Accommodation

Most hotels are concentrated in Funchal (especially the Hotel Zone – the cliff-top area, west of the town). However, there is a fair sprinkling of accommodation throughout the island. Rooms cover all price ranges – generally, the further you are from the centre of town, the less you have to pay. You may be charged extra for a sea view. There are aparthotels and other types of self-catering accommodation along the Estrada Monumental in Funchal and elsewhere on the island, especially in the Caniço area.

A small rural hotel is often called a *residencial* or *estalagem*. They are often family-run and include converted *quintas*.

Pousadas are inns owned by the Portuguese government. There are two on Madeira, both enjoying fabulous locations: one on the slopes of the Pico do Arieiro, the other in the wooded Serra da Agua Valley. Both are extremely popular and must be booked well in advance.

There is only one (small) official camp site on the island, in Porto Moniz. It is also possible to camp in the nature reserve at Montado do Pereiro, but you need a permit from the forest wardens (ask the Tourist Office in Funchal for information). There is another camp site on Porto Santo.

Eating Out

Most restaurants in Funchal are open 11:00–23:00, although some close in the late afternoon and reopen for dinner at 19:00. Many small bars stay open until 04:00. It's possible to eat well without burning a hole in your pocket. The more expensive restaurants tend to serve international cuisine, but you will find some excellent regional cooking in the mid-range establishments while everywhere there are bars and cafés serving traditional Madeiran dishes as well as a variety of snacks.

Transport

Air: Aerocondor operate internal flights from Funchal to

PUBLIC HOLIDAYS AND FESTIVALS

There are many festivals on Madeira; some are national holidays, others local celebrations of saints' days. Bands, folklore groups, decorated boats and street banners are some of the things to look out for.

1 January • New Year
February • Carnival (celebrated in towns throughout the island)
March/April • Shrove Tuesday, Ash Wednesday, Good Friday, Easter Monday
April • Flower Festival, Funchal
25 April • Day of the Revolution
1 May • Labour Day
June • Corpus Christi
10 June • National Day
1 July • Madeira Day
15 August • Feast of the Assumption (widely celebrated, especially in Monte)
21 August • Funchal Day
September • Apple Festival (Ponta do Pargo and Camacha)
September • Wine Festival (Estreito da Câmara de Lobos, Funchal and Porto da Cruz)
5 October • Republic Day
1 November • All Saints' Day, Chestnut Festival (in Curral das Freiras)
1 December • Restoration of Independence Day
8 December • Immaculate Conception
25 December • Christmas
31 December • Firework display in Funchal harbour

Porto Santo (four a day). Flight time is 15 minutes. Book well in advance in high season through a travel agent or TAP Air Portugal, 73 Apartamento

505, Avenida Arriaga,
tel: 291 235 185.

Road: Visitors cannot bring
their own cars to Madeira;
consequently there are
numerous rental firms offer-
ing competitive rates. You
can book a car in advance,
on arrival at the airport, or
through your hotel.

Avis, tel: 291 524 392 or 291
764 546.

Budget, tel: 291 524 661
or 291 764 410.

Hertz, tel: 291 523 040
or 291 003 100.

Atlantic, tel: 291 761 711.

Rodavante, tel: 291 524 718
or 291 758 506.

Atlas, tel: 291 223 100.

Drivers must be over 21 with
at least one year's experience.
Negotiating the narrow
mountain roads can be taxing,
especially when approaching
the more popular sights where
tour coaches are an additional
hazard on hairpin bends. Most
companies operate their own
breakdown services and will
explain the procedures in the
event of a breakdown. It is
essential to take out damage
waiver insurance if this is not
included in the deal.

Drive on the right-hand side
of the road and give way to
vehicles approaching from
the right. The speed limit on
motorways is 120kph
(75mph) and on urban roads
it varies from 80kph (50mph)
to 60kph (37mph), depending
on the area. It is mandatory
for drivers and passengers to
wear seat belts. Driving after
drinking more than 5mg per
litre of blood is prohibited.
Petrol is available in two
grades; lead-free and 4-star
(super). Most villages have a
garage or at least a petrol
pump (open 08:00–20:00),
but it's a good idea to fill up
before you leave Funchal.
The GALP petrol station on
Avenida do Infante is open
24 hours.

Taxis: Taxis are bright yellow
with a distinctive blue stripe
down the side. There are
ranks in every town and taxis
may also be flagged down at
the roadside. Short trips are
metered. Rates for certain
out-of-town journeys (e.g. to
the airport) are fixed and may
include waiting times. There
are surcharges for extra
luggage and for travelling

between 22:00 and 07:00,
or on Sundays and public holidays. Hourly or half-day rates
can be negotiated for longer
journeys. In Funchal taxi ranks
can be found on Avenida do
Mar, Avenida Arriaga, Largo
do Municipio and elsewhere.

Buses: There are reliable bus
connections between Funchal
and all of the main towns and
villages. Buses are modern
and comfortable and have a
good safety record. There are
a number of private opera-
tors. Municipal buses in
Funchal are orange. The main
bus stops, also ticket kiosks,
are on Avenida do Mar –
cancel your ticket in the
machine as you board the bus.
Seven-day 'go as you please'
passes are valid on all routes
and are available to visitors on
presentation of a passport.

Boats: The Porto Santo Line
ferry departs from Funchal
harbour daily around 08:00.
The journey takes about
2 hours 40 minutes. Tickets
can be bought in advance
from travel agents or from the
jetty just before sailing. For
information, contact Porto
Santo Line, rua da Praia 6,
Funchal, tel: 291 210 300.
Don't leave buying your ticket
till the last minute during high
season – there won't be any
left. Half- or full-day sightseeing cruises along the coast
leave from the yachting
marina. Sea fishing trips,
charter and evening cruises
(with dinner) are also available.

Business Hours

Shops: normal opening hours
are Monday–Friday 09:00–

CONVERSION CHART		
FROM	**TO**	**MULTIPLY BY**
Millimetres	Inches	0.0394
Metres	Yards	1.0936
Metres	Feet	3.281
Kilometres	Miles	0.6214
Square kilometres	Square miles	0.386
Hectares	Acres	2.471
Litres	Pints	1.760
Kilograms	Pounds	2.205
Tonnes	Tons	0.984
To convert Celsius to Fahrenheit: x 9 ÷ 5 + 32		

USEFUL PHRASES

hello • *olá*	*No compréndo*	where's the bus for…?	14 • *catorze*
goodbye • *adeus*	I'm lost • *Perdi-me*	• *Onde está o auto*	15 • *quinze*
good morning • *bom dia*	can you help me? • *Ajude-me, por favor*	*carro para…?*	16 • *dezasseis*
good afternoon • *boa tarde*	what time is it please? • *Que horas são, por*	1 • *um (uma)*	17 • *dezassete*
good evening /night • *boa noite*	*favor*	2 • *dois (duas)*	18 • *dezoito*
please • *se faz favor*	hotel • *hotel/estalagem*	3 • *três*	19 • *dezanove*
thank you • *obrigado/a*	bill • *conta*	4 • *quatro*	20 • *vinte*
yes • *si*	bank • *um banco*	5 • *cinco*	21 • *vinte e um*
no • *não*	can you change…? • *Pode trocar..?*	6 • *seis*	30 • *trinta*
how much is it? • *Quanto custa isto?*	post office • *correio*	7 • *sete*	40 • *quarenta*
where is the…? • *Onde fica…?*	airport • *aeroporto*	8 • *oito*	50 • *cinquenta*
I don't understand •	bus stop • *paragem*	9 • *nove*	60 • *sessenta*
	a ticket to…. • *um bilhete para…*	10 • *dez*	70 • *setenta*
		11 • *onze*	80 • *oitenta*
		12 • *doze*	90 • *noventa*
		13 • *treze*	100 • *cem/cento*
			1000 • *mil*

13:00 and 15:00–19:00 and Saturday 09:00 13:00. Larger outlets and shops in tourist areas tend to stay open through lunch and until 22:00. Shopping centres are open daily (including Sunday) 10:00–22:00. Pharmacies (*farmacia*) – look for the distinctive green cross symbol – have a 24-hour opening rota on the shop door.

Museums: opening times vary, but 10:00–12:30 and 14:30–18:00 are fairly standard. Check whether there is a closing day (often Monday) before you set out.

Business hours: Monday–Friday 09:00–17:00.

Banks: open Monday–Friday 08:30–15:00. Some open Saturday 09:00–12:30.

Main **post offices**: open Monday–Friday 08:30–20:00 and Saturday 09:00–12:30, smaller branches only open Monday–Friday 09:00–18:00. Most shops close on Sundays and public holidays. Generally, restaurants stay open, except on Christmas Day.

Time Difference

Madeira operates GMT (Greenwich Mean Time) in the summer and, along with the rest of the EU, puts the clock back one hour on the last Sunday of October and forward one hour on the last Sunday in March.

Communications

There are telephone kiosks on the main streets of Funchal and Machico. Many bars and restaurants have pay phones. Some only take phonecards that can be purchased from newsagents or on the premises, others take coins and a few even credit cards. International calls from the island are expensive, especially if made from a hotel. The international code for Madeira (Portugal) is 351 and the area code 291. There are special rates for long-distance calls between midnight and 08:00. There are post offices (*correios*) in all the main towns on Madeira and Porto Santo. The main post offices in Funchal are on Avenida do Zarco and Rua Dr Brito Câmara. They handle telegrams, telexes, faxes and telephone calls as well as mail. The main office in Porto Santo is in Vila Baleira (Avenida Vieira Castro). Postage stamps are also on sale at most newsagents.

Most European **mobile phones** work on Madeira and coverage is generally good. US phones aren't compatible, however. There are relatively few **internet cafés** on Madeira. Possibly the best is **Cremesoda Cyber Café**, rua Dos Ferreiros 9 (behind Igreja do Colegio), Funchal, tel: 291 224 920. Open Monday–Friday 09:00–21:00, Saturday 10:00–21:00, Sunday 17:00–21:00, website: www.cremesoda.com

Electricity

The power supply is 220 volts AC. Sockets are 2-pin.

Weights and Measures

Madeira uses metric weights and measurements and European clothing sizes.

Health Precautions

It is possible to burn very quickly in the Madeiran sun. Wear sunblock and if you are going to be out for a long time, cover exposed parts of your body. Tap water is safe to drink and tastes fresh. Mineral water is also widely available.

Health Services:

A visit to a doctor has to be paid for, so it's worth checking out the pharmacy first. Chemists are allowed to prescribe suitable medication – many speak a little English. If you're on medication, take supplies with you as your regular brand may not be available on the island.

In an emergency, the main hospital for foreigners is in Funchal: Cruz de Carvalho, Avenida Luis Camões. EU citizens should have form E111 to obtain a refund on basic treatment, and insurance that covers medical emergencies is also advisable for all visitors.

There are many English-speaking doctors on Madeira – ask in your hotel for the nearest. Information about English-speaking dental services in Funchal is available from hotels and tourist offices.

Personal Safety

Crime on Madeira is rare, but take the usual precautions. Deposit spare money and other valuables in the hotel safe. Do not leave valuables on the beach, at the poolside or in the car, and beware of the risk of pickpocketing in crowds. If you are the victim of theft, report it to the police and ask for a copy of the report if you intend to make an insurance claim.

The main **police station** is on Largo de São João, tel: 291 222 022.

Lost Property is at rua da Infância 28, tel: 291 208 200. If your passport goes missing you will need to get a replacement from your consulate:

UK, 2, 4° Avenida Zarco, tel: 291 221 221.

USA, Ed. Infante, Bl.B ap.B-4°, Avenida Luis Camões, tel: 291 743 429.

South Africa, Ed. Torise, Bl3, 3° R Pimenta Aguiar, tel: 291 742 825.

Emergencies

Fire, **Ambulance** and **Police**: tel: 112.
Hospital Cruz Carvalho, Funchal, tel: 291 705 600.
Hospital dos Marmeleiros, Funchal, tel: 291 705 730.
Centro de Saúde do Porto Santo, tel: 291 982 211.

Etiquette

When greeting people they know, women kiss on both cheeks, men shake hands. Dress is informal, though after dark smart-casual clothing is generally worn. Topless sunbathing is permitted in the lidos and hotel pools.

Language

Portuguese is the language of Madeira but many people working with tourists speak English, and German too. Portuguese is easier to read than to speak (especially if you know some Spanish). Madeirans will, however, appreciate any effort you make to speak their language.

GOOD READING

Cossart, N (1984) *Madeira the Island Vineyard*, Christie's Wine Publications, London.
Farrow, John and Susan (1990) *Madeira, the Complete Guide* (2nd edition), Robert Hale, London.
Liddell, Alex (1998) *Madeira*, Faber and Faber Ltd., London.
Monterey, Guido de (1998) *Madeira, Isle of Flowers* (4th edition), Jarmelos Criadores Distribuidores Graficos, Porto.
Moore, CC; Elias, G; Costa, H (1997) *Bird Watcher's Guide to Portugal and Madeira*, Prion Ltd.
Underwood, John and Pat (1999) *Landscapes of Madeira. A Countryside Guide* (5th edition). Sunflower Books, London.
Most American and English national **newspapers** are available, also a wide range of **magazines** in English. There are two island newspapers: *Jornal da Madeira* and *Diário de Notícias do Funchal*. The latter has a daily supplement in English, which includes details of TV and radio programmes in other languages.

INDEX